HALF-DAY WALKS
in
THE PEAK DISTRICT:
The South East

Alan Bradley

Published by Sigma Leisure – an imprint of
Sigma Press, 1 South Oak Lane, Wilmslow, Cheshire SK9 6AR, England.

British Library Cataloguing in Publication Data
A CIP record for this book is available from the British Library.

ISBN: 1-85058-567-9

Typesetting and Design by: Sigma Press, Wilmslow, Cheshire.

Cover photograph: Autumn view of Monsal Dale from Monsal Head (*the author*)

Photographs: The author

Sketches: Elma Bradley

Maps: The author

Printed by: MFP Design and Print

Disclaimer: the information in this book is given in good faith and is believed to be correct at the time of publication. No responsibility is accepted by either the author or publisher for errors or omissions, or for any loss or injury howsoever caused. Only you can judge your own fitness, competence and experience.

Preface

The 30 walks described in this volume are in the south-east of the Peak District, defined for this purpose as that part of the Peak National Park which lies south of the A623/619 Chapel-en-le-Frith to Chesterfield road and east of the A515 Buxton to Ashbourne road. They vary in length from 3 to 5 miles, with optional extensions.

The Peak District is the most popular of the National Parks for weekend walking, with a population of several million living within an easy drive or bus ride, and naturally there are many guides to walks of every kind. So why choose this one, or its companion volume (published 1996) dealing with the south-west of the Peak District? Here are my reasons:

1. All the walks are short - three to five miles - to suit the less strong walker, the lazy, those with young children, and those with only a limited time to spare.

2. The walks are described in detail, so that they are easily followed by those who are new to country walking or not confident in the use of maps.

3. All walks are circular, bringing you back to your car or bus stop without retracing your steps for more than a short distance (though in some cases bus users can return from a different stop).

4. The walks do not duplicate those in the most popular guidebooks (I have read quite a few) - this volume supplements those books rather than competing with them.

5. In many of the walks I have tried to introduce readers to parts of the district which even regular walkers may not know, and in particular to include paths - legitimate, of course - which are not obvious from the Ordnance Survey maps.

6. Alternative routes are given for each walk, so you can vary them to suit your requirements. Some alternatives are longer than the main route, some shorter.

7. I have excluded routes which I found obstructed, difficult to use, or just plain boring; and I point out which of the walks need dry weather or are best at a particular time of year.

8. There are notes on safe parking places and bus services, on places of interest on the way, and on amenities such as pubs which serve food, and public toilets.

9. For each walk there is a clear sketch map to supplement the text, and there are many photographs and sketches to give you an idea of the scenery.

In addition, the Introduction gives you a brief account of the landscape of this part of the Peak District and the practicalities of walking in it.

I have walked all these routes recently with my wife Elma, and I thank her for her support and help as well as for the sketches which enliven some pages of this book. The maps and photographs are my own. The cover photograph is an autumn view of Monsal Dale from Monsal Head.

I am very grateful to Roland Smith, Paul Hopkins and a number of the Rangers of the Peak Park authority. Between them they have read through a draft of the book and in many cases followed the routes described, and sent me their comments and corrections. However, any errors that remain are entirely my responsibility and I should like to hear of them, via Sigma Press.

Alan Bradley

Contents

The Walks

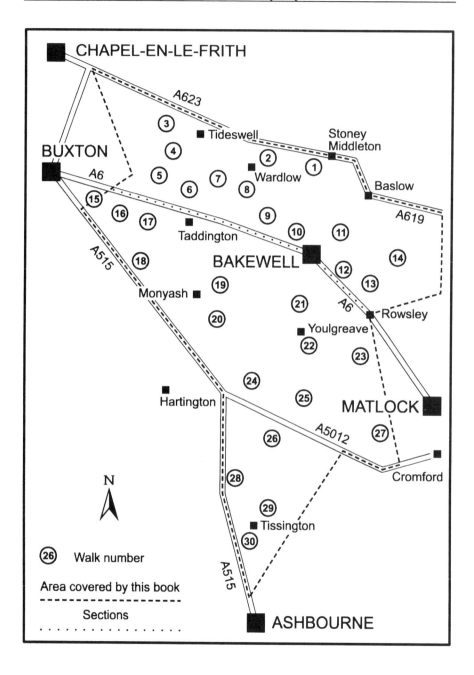

Introduction

The 'Derbyshire Dales' have long been famous for their limestone scenery, so it was natural that they should be included in the Peak National Park when this was formed in 1951. In fact the Park contains a wide range of landscapes of which the Dales are only one element. Limestone occupies less of the area of the Park than the 'Millstone Grit', a coarse sandstone which underlies the moors of the north, east and west of the Park. Furthermore, not all the Dales are in Derbyshire; the most famous of them all – Dovedale – forms the boundary between Derbyshire and Staffordshire.

This volume covers the south-eastern part of the Peak District. For convenience I have defined this as that part of the Peak National Park which lies south of the A623/A619 road from Chapel-en-le-Frith via Baslow to Chesterfield, and east of the A515 Buxton to Ashbourne road. The whole of the area is within Derbyshire. All the walks start within this area, although one or two stray across its boundary. The area contains most of the Dales, although Dovedale lies further west; it is covered in my previous volume which deals with the south-west of the Park.

Most of the area covered by this volume is limestone, although a small part of the gritstone East Moor is included. In between, the valley of the Derwent lies on the band of shale which separates the gritstone from the limestone. However there are two outcrops of gritstone west of the Derwent; Stanton Moor and Harthill Moor.

In the introduction to Volume 1, I described the basis of the Peak Park's landscape and what you should know about walking in it. I make no apology for repeating much of it here. If you are already familiar with Volume 1, you can skip most of this and start walking right away!

The National Park

The Peak Park lies within easy travelling distance of a greater population than any of the other National Parks; indeed it is said that half the population of England lives within a hour's drive, though I suspect this takes little account of traffic jams. So it is not surprising that it is the most popular of the parks – only Mount Fuji in Japan has more visitors, or so I have just been assured by the television. In a few places there are active quarries, and in many more there are traces of old mines and quarries. In spite of all this, the Park consists mostly of quiet, unspoilt countryside. Some areas are busy at summer weekends, though peaceful at other times, and the pressure of visitors has spoilt one or two tourist magnets. But there are plenty of unspoilt areas which are just as attractive to the walker, and this book aims to introduce you to some of them.

For those who do not know the area, do not expect mountains. The name 'Peak' has nothing to do with the landscape but comes from the name of a tribe that lived here in prehistoric times. Instead you will find open moorland and steep rocky valleys or 'dales', but also much farmland and many villages.

Although the moors of the north of the Park are bleak and uninhabited, most of the rest is farmed. There is very little crop growing; farming here means livestock, mainly cows and sheep. The cows need reasonably good pasture land, but sheep spend much of their lives on rough moorland, and it is their presence which preserves the moors and prevents them reverting to the woodland and scrub which covered them before man took a hand in shaping the landscape.

The Peak District National Park is administered by the Peak District National Park Authority (formerly the Peak Park Planning Board), based in Bakewell which is the Park's only town. I probably need not remind readers that National Parks in the UK, unlike many of those abroad, are not owned by the nation. Ownership of the land remains with the farmers and other landowners, and the authorities have the task of balancing the interests of the residents with those of the many visitors. Much of their work goes on 'behind the scenes' and will not be apparent to visitors, but the more public aspects include maintenance of car parks and footpaths and the running of information centres, including one in the centre of Bakewell. They publish a very useful annual broadsheet, 'Peakland Post', which is available free from all information centres within the Park and many outside it. This includes details of the opening times and charges of the tourist attractions and information centres in the Park, and also a calendar of events within or near the Park including such excitements as well-dressings, carnivals, sheepdog trials and guided walks.

Readers who want a change from walking may like to know that the Authority also runs cycle hire centres. None is within the area covered by this volume, but those on the Tissington Trail just north of Ashbourne, and the High Peak trail at Parsley Hay north of Hartington, are within a couple of miles of it. In addition, Derbyshire County Council runs a cycle hire centre at Middleton Top near Wirksworth, on the High Peak Trail about four miles outside the Park boundary. You can pick up a leaflet about it at any Peak Park Information Centre and many other Tourist Information Centres.

Although most of the land in the Park is privately owned, some of the most attractive parts are owned by the National Trust, the Peak Park Authority, and other bodies which encourage public access. They may still require you to keep to established paths, so that part of their land can serve as an undisturbed nature reserve. A large part of Chatsworth Park, though privately owned, is open to the public to walk at will; in other parts concessionary paths have been opened.

Railway Trails

One activity of the Peak Park authorities which is very visible is the conversion of several abandoned railway lines into firm paths for walkers, cyclists and horse riders. Of these, the 'Monsal Trail' is entirely within the area covered by this book. It runs from a mile south-east of Bakewell to Blackwell Cottages at the west end of Chee Dale, three miles east of Buxton. It is based on part of the former Midland Railway line from London to Manchester via Derby, which closed in the 1960s when the West Coast route was electrified; till then it offered one of the most scenic railway journeys in the country. However, there were many tunnels on the Peak District part of the route, and all but the shortest of these have been sealed off. The Monsal Trail bypasses them by using existing rights of way and a few concessionary paths, some of which are steep and narrow. For this reason the trail is little used by cyclists and horse riders, which makes it that much more comfortable for walkers. Peak Rail (an independent group) plans to restore the route for use by preserved steam trains, and it is not clear what effect that will have on walkers. However it will probably be some years before their line (which runs from Matlock to Rowsley, on the boundary of the park, at present) reaches the Monsal Trail.

Another railway trail partly within the area covered by this book is the 'High Peak Trail'. This follows the route of the very early Cromford and High Peak Railway and runs from near Cromford, entering the park some six miles on near Minninglow, to Parsley Hay (just beyond the area covered by this volume) and on to Hurdlow, south of Buxton. The railway itself continued, originally, to Whaley Bridge and served to connect the Peak Forest canal there with the Cromford canal. It consisted of near-level stretches, originally worked by horses but later by steam locomotives, linked by a number of steep inclines worked by stationary steam engines. One of these engines can still be seen (at certain times) at Middleton-by-Wirksworth just outside the Park boundary. The whole of the trail within the area of this volume is open to walkers, cyclists and horse riders.

A third railway trail, called the 'Tissington Trail' because it passes through that village, runs near the western boundary of our area and partly within it. In contrast with the High Peak line this was a railway which came very late, around the turn of the century. It was an attempt by another railway company to capture some of the London to Manchester through traffic from the Midland and LNWR railways, but had little success in that respect. However it survived until the 1960s as a branch line carrying local traffic between Uttoxeter and Ashbourne and Buxton. From Parsley Hay, north of Hartington and just outside our area, it absorbed the Cromford and High Peak railway, although that section is now regarded as part of the High Peak Trail rather than the Tissington Trail.

This trail is less scenic than the Monsal Trail but there are some good views. It is popular with cyclists, and as these don't seem to have bells any more you will need to keep a careful lookout. This trail is particularly well provided with car parks, at nearly all of the former stations, and many of them have picnic areas.

Walks along the full length of the trails are covered by various books and leaflets so I shall not repeat them here, but short sections of the trails are used in several of the walks. I have to confess that I find them a little lacking in interest for walking, though very attractive for cyclists.

Guidebooks

Peakland walks have been made better known by many footpath guides which have been published in the last twenty years. Among the best of these are the 'Pub Walks' series and other books from Sigma Press, an excellent set of three books by Mark Richards, a book of weekend walks by John and Ann Nuttall (all these from Cicerone Press), and some slim 'Family Walks' books by Norman Taylor from Scarthin Books. But all of these, except the last, concentrate on longer walks. In this book I have collected walks which suit those of us who prefer shorter walks because of our age or that of our children, or who are short of time, or just lazy;

and also beginners at country walking who are not confident of their ability to read maps. I have taken care not to duplicate any of the walks included in the books I have mentioned, although of course there is bound to be some overlap. Needless to say I have not read every guidebook, so you may yet find walks in them which correspond with mine.

The Landscape

Most of the area covered by the book is on the limestone of the 'White Peak'. On its eastern fringe is a small section of the gritstone East Moor which forms part of the 'Dark Peak', and the two are separated by a band of softer shale through which runs the valley of the river Derwent. However there are two isolated areas of gritstone west of the Derwent, forming Stanton Moor and Harthill Moor. The walks give you the opportunity to compare the contrasting landscapes associated with the three types of rock, so I shall give a very brief account of these landscapes. It is largely repeated from my previous volume, so if you have read that you can skip much of this.

The limestone country is mainly an undulating plateau cut into by steep valleys, or dales. These are often rocky and sometimes dry, with short grass and scrub or woodland. The plateau itself is farmed, almost entirely as pasture, with few trees other than shelter belts to protect farmhouses; although woodland has been planted – mostly on the steeper slopes – in the vast Chatsworth and Haddon estates. Walls are of white or pale grey limestone. The soil drains well and is usually reasonable for walking even after rain, though where the rock is exposed it can be slippery. Limestone is a valuable mineral and great quarries scar some parts of the White Peak. Most of the big quarries (especially south and east of Buxton) are excluded from the National Park, but just within our area there are active quarries at Topley Pike, three miles east of Buxton, and also near Stoney Middleton. Some large former quarries, such as those in Miller's Dale, have been landscaped by the Park authorities. Smaller quarries, long disused, exist in their hundreds. Some of these were for lime for burning to improve the soil, or for use in mortar; usually the ruins of a kiln can be seen very near by. Others were for building stone for walls or houses. Limestone is hard to work and not ideal for building, so millstone grit has often been brought from the surrounding areas for window and door surrounds and for the corners of buildings.

Winter Sunshine (Near Wardlow)

In the past these limestone areas have also produced lead. The mines are now all closed, though in one or two places the mined ground is being re-worked for other minerals. Limestone is porous (geologists, please forgive me for this simplification) and the streams often find their way underground, leaving the valleys dry. It is limestone that forms the famous Dales – including Chee Dale, Millers Dale, Monsal Dale and Lathkill Dale in our area, and others elsewhere in the White Peak – and the famous caves of Buxton and Matlock Bath (both just outside the area covered by this book) and Castleton.

Millstone grit, a coarse brown sandstone which blackens with exposure to the air, underlies the Eastern Moors and also Stanton and Harthill moors. The Eastern Moors are mainly covered by heather or by coarse grass, with rushes in the wetter patches. The west edge of these moors has spectacular cliffs further to the north, but in our area there are only minor outcrops and the escarpment is largely covered by trees. Stanton Moor is partly covered by heather and partly by scrub and small trees; there are rocky outcrops round its edges. Harthill Moor is mostly farmland, though with a few rock outcrops of which the most spectacular is 'Robin Hood's Stride'. There were quarries on Harthill Moor within recent memory; when my father wanted paving slabs to match some he already had, a local stonemason was able to tell him just which quarry they had come from and to arrange a fresh supply.

In between the limestone of the 'White Peak' and the gritstone East Moor lie the less extensive shales. These are softer and produce a gentle and reasonably fertile landscape, so practically all the areas of shale are farmed. Because the shale is soft it forms an easy course for the river Derwent. Shale is useless as a building stone, so gritstone or limestone is brought from elsewhere; walls are often replaced by hedges or fences.

The only real town within the Park is Bakewell, a small market town which caters for tourists without going overboard about them. Buxton, a larger town and former spa, was deliberately excluded from the park; Matlock, the seat of Derbyshire County Council, lies just outside it to the south-east. The villages of the Peak are mostly rural and attractive. Few of them are of any size, as judged by their ability to support more than one pub; but Tideswell is almost a small town, with quite a few shops, and formerly had a market. Baslow, Ashford and Youlgreave are also substantial villages.

I could hardly fail to mention the two great houses which ornament this section of the Park, though you would not actually include a visit to either in your walk. Chatsworth, seat of the Duke of Devonshire, is almost a byword for opulence; a showplace, magnificent but rather overwhelming in my view, though the gardens are very well worth a visit. Haddon Hall, belonging to the Duke of Rutland, is in contrast a medieval gem which time has treated lightly, and the sort of place where one could actually live (with an army of servants, of course). Its gardens are also very fine though totally different from Chatsworth. It is worth seeing both, if only for the contrast between them. Opening hours are listed in 'Peakland Post' as well as the usual tourist guides. Both are closed in the winter.

Peak District buildings are mostly in the local limestone or gritstone, thanks to the planning control exercised by the Peak Park board, and blend well with the landscape. Stone walls are very much a feature of the park, and while some are disused and derelict, most are well maintained. Often the clearest indication that you are crossing the boundary between gritstone and limestone is a change in the colour of the field walls, because walling stone was never carried far. Besides the lie of the land itself, it is buildings, walls and trees that create the characteristic landscape of the Peak.

The Walks

All the walks in this book are between three and five miles in length, although they may include a fair amount of ascent and descent. In all cases two to three hours (plus any stops) should be enough for the average to slow walker. I have tried to distinguish between walks which need dry weather and those which are passable even after rain, though of course I have not walked every route in every season. Conditions in this part of the Peak do not compare with those on the northern moors or in mountains, but rain can come unexpectedly and the winter wind can be very cold. In winter I would certainly recommend boots for most of these walks, because muddy patches are unavoidable. There should be no need for compass, whistle and survival bag; but don't forget your waterproofs and a warm jumper – and the thermos if you are one of those who need tea or coffee to keep you going.

In very dry weather it is occasionally necessary to close some areas of moor because of fire or the risk of it. Very occasionally, the authorities have had to ban or at least discourage walking in some areas – particularly farmland – because of animal diseases such as foot-and-mouth. If you come across such restrictions, please observe them – your short cut may make the difference between life and death for a whole herd of cattle.

Several of the walks pass through nature reserves. Although walkers are not discouraged (and in some cases there are concessionary paths in addition to the rights of way), you should keep to the paths to avoid disturbing wild life or damaging vegetation. In particular, never pick wild flowers or dig up plants – in fact you could be prosecuted for doing this anywhere in the Park. Of course you are welcome to take photographs.

Simply for convenience in listing the walks and drawing the key map, I have divided the walks into two groups; respectively north-east and south-west of the A6 Buxton to Matlock road. Within each group the walks are numbered roughly from north to south. This brings adjacent walks together in most cases, in case you would like to combine them. With minor exceptions the main routes do not overlap, but some of the alternative routes do.

I have walked or re-walked all the walks in this book, with my wife Elma, over the last couple of years. We have walked at all times of year – in the spring, when the trees are coming into leaf and the limestone flowers are at their best; in the summer when everything is verdant but foliage sometimes obscures the view; in the autumn when the heather and the turning leaves give the finest colouring; and in winter when frost or snow can transform the landscape and freeze mud and puddles solid. All seasons have their attractions, but in spite of the weather we find the Peak at its best in the off-season rather than the height of summer. Try it and see what you think.

Maps

I have included a sketch map of each walk. These vary slightly in scale, and sometimes in orientation, to fit them on the page; but in all cases the scale and north point are clearly shown. I have shown public roads and relevant car parks, and have distinguished between the main route and alternative routes described in the text. Other paths (not necessarily rights of way), and details such as buildings and woods, are shown only where relevant to route finding. I have not shown walls and fences; there are so many that the map would be very cluttered by them. Nor have I shown bridges or stepping stones. You can take it for granted that where the route crosses water, there is a dry way across: if there may be problems in wet weather, the text will say so. In places I have distorted the scale to show details more clearly (incidentally, all distances in the text are approximate). The maps are intended to supplement the text rather than replace it, and to help you find the starting point and relate the route to Ordnance Survey maps. I have numbered a few key points in the text and on the maps to help you to relate the two, and sometimes to show more clearly where alternative routes diverge and rejoin. These points are simply numbered in sequence, they do not indicate any particular distance.

With these sketch maps and the text there should be no difficulty in following the route. Nevertheless I strongly recommend that you carry a good map, preferably the Ordnance Survey Outdoor Leisure 'White Peak' map at a scale of 1 to 25,000 (4 centimetres to the kilometre, or about 2½ inches to the mile). This will not only let you make your own variations on the routes I give, perhaps to suit a different parking spot or to make the walk longer or shorter; it will also tell you a great deal about your surroundings, and in particular the contours will show you the relief of the countryside. The great merit of this map for walkers is that it shows field boundaries, essential if you are following a path without a detailed guide. Don't forget that a path shown as a right of way may be impassable in practice, though it certainly ought not to be.

One word of advice: this is a double-sided map, and it is almost impossible to reverse it in a high wind – difficult enough in a car. So make sure it is right way round before you leave home. Most of the walks in this volume are on the 'East' side of the sheet.

Supposing that you have a map and are at home with it, you could find your own walks; what more has a book like this to tell you? Quite a lot, I believe. Firstly, the map shows rights of way but does not distinguish between the ones which are easy walking and those which are muddy, overgrown or obstructed. Secondly there is the 'white road' problem. One of the few weaknesses of OS maps (although there are signs that the OS has begun to recognise it at last) is that a pair of parallel lines, solid or broken, with white between them may be a public road, a private drive or farm track, or occasionally even a stream bed. Sometimes you can tell that a 'white road' is public because rights of way end on it, but this doesn't always help; the only conclusive answer is to look at the 'definitive maps' held by the Park authorities and county council. Thirdly there are some paths which are not rights of way but where there is formal or informal acceptance of public use – only a few recognised 'concessionary paths' appear on the map. Fourthly, apart from official car parks the map does not show where it is safe (and acceptable) to park. And lastly the map does not tell you which paths are attractive and which are boring, although the skilled map reader will find some clues.

The one-inch to the mile Ordnance Survey 'Peak District touring map and guide' is also an excellent map, and I recommend it for finding your way to the start of these walks. It is layer-contoured, so gives a better idea of the lie of the land to those who are not at home with contour lines. It shows footpaths (though those whose eyesight is less than perfect will find them hard to see), but I cannot recommend it as a footpath map because it does not show field boundaries, and it is often vital that you know which side of a fence to look for the path. However, the directions in this book should solve that sort of problem for you, so the one-inch map is an adequate companion. If you are familiar with the red-covered 1:50,000 'Landranger' OS maps, note that the one-inch map is on a slightly smaller scale. Incidentally, on my copy of this map the emphasised grid lines are not at the usual '0' and '5' points; if yours is the same, don't get caught out.

I have given grid references (two letters followed by six figures) for the starting points of all walks. If you are not familiar with the National Grid system, which allows you to identify any point in the UK, I strongly recommend you to learn how to use it. It is easy enough, and you will find full instructions on your Ordnance Survey map. Briefly, the letters identify a large area and in fact are SK for every point in this book, so you can ignore them. The first two figures identify a vertical grid line on your map (the lines are one kilometre apart on 1:25,000, 1:50,000 and one-inch maps alike). The third figure tells you how far across the space between this grid line and the next your point is; for example a 3 means that it is three-tenths of the way (in other words 300 metres) to the right (east) of the line you have identified. The remaining three figures are used in exactly the same way but with the horizontal grid lines and the distance northwards from a line. The only vital thing to remember is that East comes before North – easy if you know your alphabet.

Paths and stiles

The walks described follow rights of way or recognised concessionary footpaths, with a very few exceptions. On these few I found the paths clear, well-used and unobstructed. I cannot promise that they will be available to you, but I should be surprised if they were not. The descriptions of the walks make it clear which paths these are. Concessionary footpaths may of course be closed, although this is most unusual. Rights of way should be unobstructed and I have found them so as far as the walks in this book are concerned. If you do find an obstruction, you will do future walkers a service if you report it to any Peak Park information office, or to the Ramblers Association who will know what action to take. Remember that muddy patches and animals are not legally an obstruction, not even bulls if these are with dairy herds – all these animals are harmless. Young cows and bullocks are very curious and may gather round you, but they will not harm you and will back off when you approach them. Sheep, especially any that have been hand-reared, may try to share your sandwiches if given a chance. Farm dogs (and occasionally geese) can be alarming, but even so I have never been attacked by one. They are normally trained to know where the public is tolerated, and will do no more than bark if you keep to the path and show by your behaviour that you are confident of your right to be there.

Those who are new to this part of the country will find that a Peak District stile is not usually the wooden rail-and-plank structure of more southerly counties, although there are some of these. It is more likely to be a narrow gap, flanked by large stones, in a stone wall (a 'squeezer stile'), or stone steps built into each side of the wall ('step stile') – these can be difficult to spot from a distance; or occasionally a pair of wooden ladders leading over the wall ('ladder stile'). When there is no stile but only a gate, open this rather than climbing it if possible. On a 'bridle path' the gate should definitely be able to be opened, and usually can be. On a 'footpath' you may have to climb, although the official line is that "it is not acceptable that walkers should have to climb gates on a public footpath, and any locked gates should be reported to the County Council". There is a wide variety of fastenings, ranging from a loop of string or even barbed wire to metal fasteners of Chinese Puzzle standard, but a little ingenuity will deal with most of them. You will often need to lift the catch end of the gate to open it even when the catch is undone. Remember to leave the gate fastened if you found it so.

Most but by no means all footpaths are signposted where they leave a public road, which may be just a track rather than tarmac, and you will sometimes find signposts elsewhere. The most popular paths are waymarked with small yellow arrows or just blobs of yellow paint (sometimes light blue for a bridleway); this will be done especially if a footpath has been legally diverted to a new route, for example to avoid a farmyard. But many paths are not marked in any way, so you must depend on a guidebook like this or a large scale map. If in doubt about the right way through a farm, ask anyone who is in sight. The farmer will appreciate your asking rather than pressing on, and will probably be glad to pass the time of day with you. But don't argue about rights of way with a farmer; route changes may take some time to appear on maps, and in any case you can't win even if he is wrong! So always be courteous to farmers and they will usually forgive you for your mistakes, real or imagined. I have only once encountered a really angry farmer (in a different National Park), and he was clearly unwell and retired soon afterwards.

A quick word about rights of way for those who are not familiar with the term. These are routes where the public's right to walk has been established by long tradition, or occasionally by agreement. That right is now explicitly protected by law, and a right of way can only be closed or re-routed after a legal process which is difficult and so rarely exercised. Where a legal diversion does occur you should find it very clearly indicated by signs, though it may take a couple of years to appear on maps. Ordnance Survey maps show rights of way (green broken lines on the 1:25,000 map, red on smaller scales); there may be different versions, such as 'footpaths' and 'bridle ways' but there is no practical difference to walkers. A further type is the 'byway open to all traffic' which is theoretically open to vehicles as well as walkers, although in some cases quite impracticable for wheeled traffic. Until recently these were not shown as such (sometimes not shown at all) on OS maps; on the most recent 1:25,000 map I find that some, but by no means all, do appear.

You have the right to pass along a right of way whether it is visible on the ground or not, even (in single file) if it crosses crops. The farmer is required to re-level a pathway after ploughing over it, though this doesn't always happen; in this case you may find it easier to go round the edge of the field than across it. Sometimes the landowner suggests a diversion without legal powers – for example, round a garden or farmyard rather than through it – and in that case it would be courteous to follow it if it is reasonably passable, though you are not obliged to do so. If a right of way is obstructed you are legally entitled to remove as much of the obstruction as is necessary to pass, but I would not advise you to do so if you can find another legal way round – report it to the authorities and let them sort it out. If you stick to the routes in this book you should not have this problem.

A right of way is only a right of passage. You are not legally entitled to play games, pick crops (such as mushrooms), or picnic, though if you use common sense you are unlikely to meet any objections. Most farmers accept gracefully the public's right to use rights of way across their land. A few resent it, and while they cannot prevent you passing they are entitled to be strict about your keeping precisely to the right of way and to the rules.

Transport

Most walkers reach their starting point by car these days, and I have indicated safe parking places at the start of each walk – sometimes a choice, for the benefit of people coming to the area from different directions. (I mean safe from a traffic point of view; unfortunately thieves have been known to visit rural car parks, so lock your car and do not leave anything tempting in sight). Do take care not to park where you may obstruct the road or a farm gate, however little it looks to be used, and don't park in passing places on narrow roads. Don't park in what looks like a lay-by opposite a farm gate either, the farmer may need the space to swing round with a large trailer. Open grassland alongside an unfenced road usually counts as farm land rather than part of the road, and parking will not be welcomed by the farmer. If you follow the directions in this book you should not have this sort of problem.

There are reasonable bus services in this part of the Park and most walks can be reached this way, though you may have to change buses on the way and you need to take some care over your timing. Where I believe that a bus service may be useful, I have mentioned it. In particular you may find a use for the special ramblers' services which run on summer weekends. I have not given bus times or route numbers, because many services change from time to time. Derbyshire County Council publish a complete timetable of all bus and train services in the Peak District (including those outside Derbyshire itself) twice a year, with updates in between. This is obtainable from Peak Park information centres and from the Public Transport Unit, Derbyshire County Council, Chatsworth Hall, Chesterfield Road, Matlock DE4 3FW; at the time of writing it costs £1.20 including postage. It is essential reading for those without their own transport, and also useful if you want to plan a walk that does not return to its starting point. For individual services you can enquire by telephone; ring Busline on Buxton (01298) 23098.

No railways remain in the part of the National Park covered by this book, but there is a regular service to Buxton from Manchester and beyond, and to Matlock from Derby; also trains on the Sheffield to Manchester line which connect at Hope with some of the buses serving our area. These rail services are included in the timetable mentioned above.

Peak Rail, the railway conservation group which hopes eventually to restore the route from Matlock through Bakewell to Buxton, at present runs some steam trains from Matlock to Darley Dale (south of Rowsley). Before too long the route should be extended to Rowsley and on into the Park, and thus become useful to walkers, but this may not happen during the currency of this book. In the past they have also run occasional trains from Buxton to Blackwell Cottages at the end of Chee Dale. Your local Tourist Information Office should be able to tell you the situation.

Eating

Any of these walks can be completed in half a day, and we have often found it convenient to take a morning walk and then find lunch at a quiet pub. One of the happiest developments of the last couple of decades has been the spread of lunchtime catering to country pubs, especially in areas like the Peak. So I have mentioned suitable pubs near to each walk. Most of them we have visited and enjoyed; a few of those mentioned I have not visited, but I know from other sources that food is available. At all the pubs I mention there is lunchtime food both at weekends and during the week, but a few publicans have a day off during the week, so be prepared to try elsewhere if necessary. I have not generally looked for pubs actually on the route of the walk, partly for this reason and partly because muddy boots are not always welcome – though one couple I saw recently had solved this problem by putting tough plastic bags over their boots as they entered. Children are welcome at most pubs at lunchtime nowadays, if not always in the evening. There are a few cafes in this area, but nowadays the sign 'Farmhouse teas' has become rare – no doubt something to do with EC food hygiene regulations.

Remember that landlords and cooks change from time to time. I cannot promise that your lunch will be as good as mine was, nor that the attitude to children will be the same. If you are disappointed by the meal (or if you particularly enjoy it), tell the landlord and not me! On the other hand, if you find that a pub has given up serving lunchtime food or excludes children, I should like to hear of it (via the publisher) so that I can correct any future edition.

I am no connoisseur of ale, so this is not a 'Pub walks' guide in the sense of the series published by Sigma. I enjoy a drink to help my lunch down, but on the whole I judge a pub by its ability to serve good simple hot food, reasonably promptly, in a friendly (and not too smoky) atmosphere. A few country pubs have moved up-market, and turned themselves into fashionable restaurants. Good luck to them; but this is not the sort of pub I look for when I am out walking.

Pub opening hours have become more variable since the regulations were eased, but at most pubs that supply food you will be able to eat between noon and 2 pm, and after 6 (sometimes 7) in the evening; some have longer hours. At other times when the pub is open you may be able to get cold snacks as well as drinks, but don't bank on finding anything very filling.

Safety and Courtesy

There are many abandoned mineshafts in the Peak District. Most of them have been made safe, but a few have not. Don't let your children get too near, because the ground may crumble. A conical depression may be a run-in mineshaft; again, most are safe, but it's better not to take a risk. You may find horizontal mine tunnels ('adits' or 'levels') or natural caves that are open too. Treat these with caution; if you must venture in, don't go further than you can see. Remember that there may be shafts in the floor of the tunnel, sometimes hidden by rotten wood, or boulders dangerously balanced above you. Better to take your children to one of the mines or caves that are open to the public – for example at Castleton, Buxton or Matlock Bath.

I have not taken a dog on any of these walks. If you do, please make sure that it is on a lead whenever there are other animals in sight – they may be harmed if scared by the sight of even the most placid dog.

If you have small children, for their own safety do make sure that they are close to you when there are animals about. Take especial care near crags and rivers. Teach your children to watch out for barbed wire, and don't let them climb on walls, fences or gates: they may well hurt themselves and they will certainly not please the farmer. Occasionally a gate on a public footpath is padlocked or otherwise fixed, and you will have to climb over. Make sure your children know that they should climb at the hinge end of the gate, to avoid damaging it.

And finally, follow the countryside code, which is really just common sense – don't disturb animals, don't trample crops, don't start fires, leave gates as you find them (unless a gate is open which should obviously be shut, for example to keep animals off the road), don't damage walls or fences or obstruct lanes or gateways, and in particular remember that the countryside is the farmer's livelihood as well as his home. With very few exceptions, country people are friendly people; but one thoughtless walker can queer the pitch for the many that follow.

Enjoy your walking!

Note for readers of Volume 1

If you have Volume 1 of this series, covering the south-west of the Peak Park, there are a few corrections and amendments that you may like to note.

Walk 1: the latest (double sided) edition of the Ordnance Survey 'Dark Peak' map covers a larger area and does include the route of this walk. The National Trust proposes to restore the Cage.

Walk 7: the pastoral scene illustrated is not on this walk but in limestone country.

Walk 9: at Sparbent, improvements to the main road have involved providing a ladder stile rather than steps after you cross the road. The path is indicated by a signpost.

Walks 10, 12 and 13: the Fourways Diner is not at present open for meals.

Walk 16: the photograph was actually taken on Walk 20 near Redhurst Crossing.

Walks 17 and 18: there are now toilets and a small visitor centre, displaying the history of the Manifold Valley Light Railway, near the Hulme End car park.

Walk 20: in the second paragraph under 'Alternative routes', after passing the car park go straight on instead of turning RIGHT.

Walk 23: some friends following this walk were unwilling to go on when they found clay pigeon shooting going on across the right of way. The official line on this is "It is not an offence to shoot across a public footpath although to do so could be in breach of the Health and Safety at Work Act 1974 or an obstruction and intimidation of users of the path under Section 130 of the highways act 1980. If you do believe there is a danger from a shoot taking place in the vicinity of a footpath then I suggest that you inform the Highway Authority, Derbyshire county Council." This is not much help if you are on the spot; I suggest that you shout or wave or otherwise attract the attention of the shooters, and wait for someone who is in charge to wave you on.

Walk 28: the Newhaven Inn is at present closed and semi-derelict, although the Park authorities are making efforts to have it restored. The Jug and Glass, a mile or so further north on the A515, was also closed when I passed recently.

Walk 1: Stoney Middleton and Coombs Dale

Start: At Lane Head (SK212751), a mile west of Stoney Middleton on the minor road (south of the A623) which runs over the moor to the Cavendish Mill. Lane Head is the point where the road crosses a small dip, and firm tracks run both uphill and downhill. If you come from the west, you will find signs in the industrial surroundings of Cavendish Mill (SK205752) to distinguish the road from the many industrial tracks.

There is no car park, but there are several places just west of Lane Head where cars can be parked on the verge. Take care not to block gateways or passing places.

You can also park in Eyam village. The car park is at the west end of the village so this will add half a mile to your walk, but it will be an interesting half mile even though you will be returning by the same route. However the village and the car park are likely to be very busy at summer weekends.

Distance: 4½ miles (alternatives 3 and 5 miles).

Public transport: Buses between Buxton and (alternately) Chesterfield or Sheffield run hourly along Middleton Dale and Eyam Dale, and on Friday to Sunday there are a few buses from Manchester. On summer Sundays there is a single bus from Rochdale and Oldham.

Amenities: There are pubs and cafes in Eyam and Stoney Middleton. Public toilets in Eyam, at the west end of the village (a quarter of a mile from the route of the walk).

The walk starts on the moors, crosses Middleton Dale and follows Eyam Dale to the outskirts of the village, then runs across fields to the village of Stoney Middleton. It climbs out of the village and descends into Coombs Dale, returning by way of Black Harry Lane.

The walk is entirely on limestone and there has been extensive quarrying in this area. An active quarry is passed near the beginning of the walk. Until recently there was mining in Coombs Dale, but that has now ceased; the landscape has been restored and nature will soon complete the task. The dale is dry and partly wooded, with some rock in the sides although less than in the better known dales.

The walk should be passable in any weather. About half a mile of the

Tollhouse at Stoney Middleton

walk is on roads, but these are not usually busy although summer weekends bring more traffic to Eyam Dale.

The scale of the sketch map is distorted at Eyam and Stoney Middleton in order to show the route more clearly.

The Walk

Take the walled lane leading downhill from the road at Lane Head. Although tarmac, this is not now used by vehicles. Ignore side turnings and stiles. The lane is rural at first but shortly runs between two quarries, still in use, and becomes a path running alongside a quarry track. At the bottom of the hill, where you reach quarry buildings, cross the track and go down a stony path (with an inconspicuous footpath sign) to the left of the buildings. This brings you quickly to the A623 main road running through Middleton Dale.

Cross the road carefully and walk up the road opposite, signposted to Eyam. The footway ends after two hundred metres, but the road is broad and not usually busy. This is Eyam Dale. As you enter the village of Eyam, keep right at two road junctions (the village centre is to the left; it is well known to tourists. If you want to visit it, return to this point afterwards).

1. STONEY MIDDLETON AND COOMBS DALE

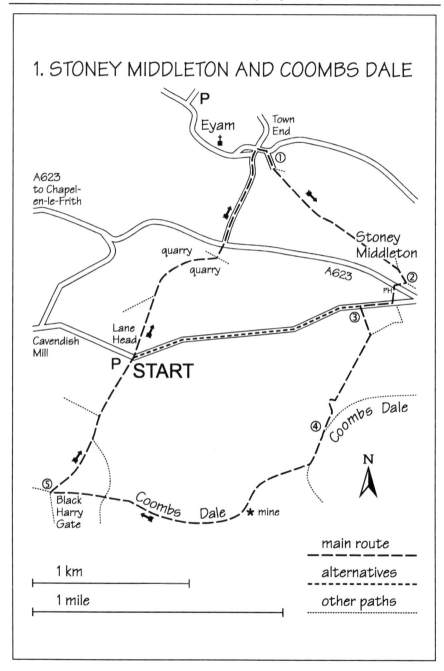

Turn right at a telephone kiosk and pillar box **(1)** into Lydgate, a tarmac lane. In about two hundred metres the tarmac bears left; go straight ahead through a squeezer stile beside an iron gate (with a footpath sign) and continue, past a few houses, on a clear track. At the end of the field go straight ahead through a squeezer stile (with signpost and waymark) and along a walled footpath below old mine buildings.

The next stile brings you into a large open field. Go straight ahead, aiming just right of a tree-topped mound. Go straight on, between two small ridges – do not drop into the valley on the left. When houses come in sight, aim for them, and you will come to a stile in the bottom corner of the field. Cross it and turn right along the tarmac lane, with houses on your left. Shortly you will be able to see the unusual octagonal church at the end of Stoney Middleton village.

At the junction of lanes, just past a telephone box **(2)**, turn sharp right down to the octagonal toll house. This is now a fish and chip shop, but probably closed at this time of day; however there are seats in the little park alongside where you can rest your legs and perhaps enjoy a picnic. Then cross the main road and go up the tarmac footpath opposite, leaving the Royal Oak inn to your right.

At the top of the path, turn right up the very steep lane, between houses. If you stayed on the lane you would be back at Lane Head in a mile; but for Coombs Dale, look out for a stile on your left where the slope eases and there is a long gap between houses **(3)**. Go over the stile, signposted 'Great Longstone', and along the field to the next signpost. Beyond the squeezer stile turn half right across the field in the direction indicated by the signpost, aiming for Coombs Dale which you can now see ahead of you.

After four more squeezer stiles (some are a very tight squeeze) the path descends steeply through scrub and then curves round the head of a tiny side valley. You are now on rocks above Coombs Dale, and the path descends the second of two little gulleys; there is a clear path, but you will probably find the grass to the right of it is easier going. The path curves to the right and runs parallel to the dale bottom for some way before joining it at a wooden gate **(4)**.

Go through the gate and turn right along the track, a disused mine road. Now just follow Coombs Dale for a mile. Half-way along you will come to the derelict buildings of Sallet Hole mine, if they have not been tidied away, with the large entrance tunnel (blocked) behind them to your left. Beyond this point there used to be a very broad firm mine track up the dale, but when I went that way at the end of 1995 most of its width was being covered with soil to leave a narrow path which I am told is firm and dry.

The dale sides gradually become lower. In half a mile you will pass stiles on each side of the track and an iron gate, and then shortly come to a crossing of tracks **(5)** with a signpost (rickety, so you may find it missing). Go up the walled bridle path on the right – this is Black Harry Lane, signposted to Stoney Middleton and Eyam. As it reaches the top of the hill there is a high bank on your left. This is a large settling lagoon associated with the Cavendish Mill, which has been completely filled and grassed over. The path becomes a track, and leads in a short distance back to Lane Head.

Alternative routes

The minor road between Lane Head and Stoney Middleton gives you the opportunity to leave out either Eyam Dale or Coombs Dale, reducing the distance to a little over 3 miles in each case. If you take the lane towards Stoney Middleton, you will pass several houses before you come to the stile on your right, but do not enter the continuously built up area.

You can if you wish walk along the main A623 road directly from the foot of Eyam Dale to Stoney Middleton; the road is busy, but there is a footway alongside.

If you want to walk a bit further, I suggest you explore the attractive and historic village of Eyam.

Walk 2: Wardlow and Upper Cressbrook Dale

Start: At the large car park on the north side of the A623 at Housley (SK193760), just east of the Foolow turning and less than a mile east of the junction with B6465 at Wardlow Mires. The car park is used by HGVs on weekdays, when there is usually a mobile snack bar, but is quiet at weekends.

Alternatively, a few cars can park on the grass verge near the junction at Wardlow Mires. It is difficult to park in Wardlow village, or on the minor roads crossed by this walk.

Distance: 5 miles (alternatives 2¼ to 6 miles).

Public transport: There are a few buses through Wardlow Mires and Wardlow village on the Bakewell – Tideswell – Castleton route, though not on winter Sundays.

On weekdays there are buses approximately every two hours on the Sheffield to Buxton and Chesterfield to Buxton routes passing through Foolow village, about a third of a mile from the route of the walk north of Houseley.

On summer Sundays there is a single bus, timed to suit ramblers, from Rochdale, Oldham and Glossop to Bakewell and Matlock; this passes Housley and Wardlow Mires.

Amenities: The Bull's Head in Wardlow village serves hot food at lunchtime ('Ramblers please use the back entrance', where you can leave your boots). I am told that the Three Stag's Heads inn at Wardlow Mires now offers good food; there is a cafe by the filling station opposite. There is often a mobile snack bar at the Housley car park.

If you go through Foolow and up to Bretton you can eat, and admire the view, at the Barrel Inn. Tideswell has several cafes and inns; my preference is the unpretentious Horse and Jockey, set back from the wide main street. There are also pubs and cafes in Eyam, which may be busy at weekends as it is popular with tourists.

There are public toilets behind the bus shelter in the main street at Tideswell, and at the car park in Eyam.

The walk starts at the hamlet of Housley on the A623 and crosses the fields to Wardlow before dropping into Cressbrook Dale. It follows the upper part of the dale, passing the Peter Stone, to Wardlow Mires and

The Peter Stone, Crossbrook Dale

then returns across the fields to Housley. The walk is entirely on limestone.

This part of Cressbrook Dale is less well known than the lower section but is just as attractive. It is normally dry and is clear of trees, with craggy sides. From one side rises the impressive Peter Stone, an isolated crag which you can scramble up to if you wish. The dale is a good place for wild flowers in the spring. In my opinion, the view of Cresswell Dale from the Wardlow path is one of the best in the district.

There is about a quarter mile of road walking, mostly along a quiet byway; on the busier stretch there is a footway beside the road. The walk should be possible in all weathers. A section of the dale can flood after heavy rain, but it should be possible to avoid this by walking a little higher up the dale side. The farmyard at Wardlow Mires and the path beyond it may have muddy patches, so boots are advisable.

The Walk

Cross the road from the Housley car park and enter the drive opposite the Foolow road, but immediately go over a step stile on the right (signposted to Great Longstone) and turn left alongside the wall. Cross two more stiles and then head half right diagonally across a large field, aiming for the right-hand edge of a copse. Cross a step stile with a footpath signpost, and go on in the same direction across the next field

2. WARDLOW AND UPPER CRESSBROOK DALE

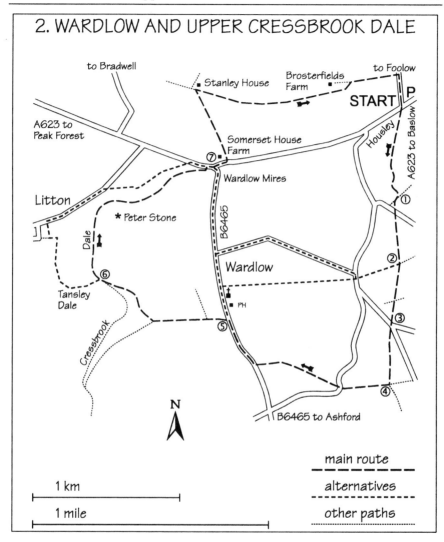

and through a gateway. Follow the wall round to the left, and then diverge from it and go over a wooden stile in the far corner of a field onto a farm lane **(1)**.

Go over the step stile opposite and half right across the field to another stile, and onto the road. Go straight across, through a stile by a broken footpath signpost (maybe someone will have mended it). Go half left – there is a faint path visible – and over an inconspicuous step stile in the left wall. Go on in the same direction, over another step stile about twenty metres left of the field corner, and on over a wooden stile in a wire fence **(2)**.

Beyond this you could turn right for one of the alternative routes, but for the main route go straight on over another wooden stile to yet another stile, just right of a post. This brings you onto a track between a fence and a wall (not obvious on the OS map – there has been much re-organisation of walls and fences around here). Cross the track, go through the wall gap and through a gate, then turn half right through another wall gap to a wicket gate. This brings you onto a road, close to a junction **(3)**.

Cross the road and go over a step stile opposite, with a footpath signpost. Go half left across the field, well left of a wide wall gap, to a decrepit step stile visible as a notch in the wall (unless it has been mended). Go straight on to a similar stile, at an angle where the wall steps forward a few metres. Continue over the remains of old mine workings towards a pair of posts, go over the step stile between them **(4)**, and turn right along a track parallel to the wall. (You could avoid a few stiles by turning left along the last road you came to, forking right, and then turning right at a footpath sign onto the track alongside the wall).

The track leads through more old mine workings, then downhill towards a gate. A stile in the field corner, to the right of the gate, brings you onto a road and you can see Wardlow village ahead of you.

Cross the road and go through the signposted squeezer opposite. The path is probably clear on the ground, but I cannot be sure because there was snow on the ground when we went this way. Go down the field, past capped mine shafts, to a wooden stile just left of the lowest part of the field. Go straight ahead, more or less level along the hillside, to a wooden stile where a wire fence meets the wall (beware of barbed wire). Keep on, rising slowly, past an electricity pole and a hawthorn bush, alongside a ruined wall, and left of a tree to a stile by a wooden gate. This brings you onto the B6465 road.

Turn right down the road into Wardlow village; there is a footway alongside. Before reaching the dip (and well before the Bull's Head, which you can see ahead) turn left, opposite a converted barn, into a walled track signposted 'Ravensdale' **(5)**. At a junction, go through a squeezer and straight ahead along a walled path. This ends at a stile overlooking Cressbrook Dale. Pause to admire the fine view of this curving dale, with Litton village beyond it. Most of the dale is a nature reserve, as a signboard will tell you. This is a grand picnic spot if there isn't a strong wind – odd how the English always react to a good view by feeling hungry!

Go forward a few metres to a waymark post and turn right on the path which slopes down the hillside into the dale. This can be slippery in places, though a good deal of work has been done to improve the worst parts. At the bottom **(6)**, the main path goes over a stile on the left and up Tansley Dale to Litton; but your way is straight ahead, along the bottom of the dale.

The craggy sides of the dale are impressive, and where it bends right you can see a rocky peak like a miniature mountain on your right. This is the Peter Stone. You will see it better by looking back from further up the dale (though photographers will wish they could remove a prominent house from the background – artists can do that if they wish). If you feel the need to climb it, follow a faint path between the Stone and the dale side and climb to the top from there. Tradition says that one of the last public hangings in Derbyshire took place on the Peter Stone; it would be hard to choose a more prominent place.

The rocky dale sides eventually give way to grass and you see the A623 main road ahead, but the path curves right and passes through a yard before meeting the road at Wardlow Mires. (If this stretch is very muddy, you can cross a broken wall at the dale end to reach the road at a stile, by a signpost, a hundred or so metres further left).

Turn right, cross the side road to Wardlow **(7)** and pass in front of the inn, then turn left into a farmyard. The way through this was clearly signed when I passed; it is left, just right of a flight of steps on the end of a barn, then right alongside a wall and through a wooden wicket gate. Now go straight up two fields with the wall on your left. At the third field, go straight ahead to Stanley House but do not go over the stile in front of it; instead, turn right alongside the wall.

Now continue across several fields, keeping the wall on your left although some of the stiles in cross-walls are a few metres to the right of it. Pass to the right of a barn. Shortly there is a farm over to your left, and the wall ends at a signpost pointing the way you came. Go straight ahead to a stile beside an iron gate and along the farm drive beyond it. This soon brings you to a road. Turn right along it, and where it approaches the main road in about 300 metres, turn left into the Housley car park.

Alternative routes

You can save about half a mile on the way into Wardlow village if you turn right after the third stile (the first wooden one) after crossing the first minor road. Walk down the field alongside the wire fence and cross a wooden stile to reach a road between two junctions.

For the driest way to Wardlow go a few metres to the right and turn left down a minor road, and turn left when you reach Wardlow to rejoin the main route. Otherwise go over a step stile beside the gate opposite you, and down a long field past old mine workings. When I last went this way the upper part of the field was being levelled and was muddy, but by now the grass may have grown again – you should be able to see from the road.

As you go down the field, aim for the left-hand wall where it disappears over the ridge, and follow it down to a concrete slab stile just right of a tree, and on through a wall gap. Now follow the wall on your right. When you pass another wall gap you will see a short wall pointing towards you in the dip. Go just left of it to a stile in the wall angle. Now go up another field disturbed by mining, keeping towards the left to avoid the worst of the mud, and walk just right of a graveyard to join the road by a telephone box. Turn left, past the Bull's Head, and take a walled path signposted 'Ravensdale' on the right opposite a converted barn. You are now back on the main route.

You could save three quarters of a mile by following the A623 from Wardlow Mires back to Housley, but this involves walking for three quarters of a mile along a busy road. Of course, if you are using the bus you can avoid this.

For a short walk of about 2¼ miles, park on the verge near Wardlow Mires (or use the bus), walk up the road into Wardlow Village and look out for the Ravensdale footpath on the right beyond the Bull's Head. Follow the main route from there.

For a longer walk, you can go by way of Litton village and see the upper part of Cressbrook Dale and the Peter Stone from the dale rim instead of the dale bottom. This will add about a mile to the walk.

To follow this route, when you reach the bottom of Cressbrook Dale you should follow the main footpath to the left up Tansley Dale. At a walled track, turn left and then right into Litton, a very attractive little village built around a green. Turn right along the road and over the brow of the hill. From here you have a fine view down into Cressbrook Dale, with the Peter Stone opposite. Where the dale and the road part company, go through a stile on the right and down the path to Wardlow Mires. Walk carefully right along the road, past the inn, to regain the main route.

Walk 3: Wheston, Peter Dale and Hay Dale

Start: Park on the broad grass verge of the road leading north from Wheston (SK133764) to Peak Forest, south of the point (SK128778) where the Limestone Way joins the road. You will be walking along this road so it does not matter exactly where you park, but if you choose a place not too far from Wheston it will divide the road walking between the start and end of your walk. In very wet weather, when the verge is too soft for parking, park at the roadside in Wheston village.

You cannot park where the road west from Wheston crosses the dale, and there is very little space where the road west from Monksdale House crosses the dale (and cars left there spoil the view). However you can park on the verge between Wheston and Monksdale house.

One of the alternative routes starts from Tideswell.

Distance: 4½ miles (alternatives 3 to 6).

Public transport: None very close to the main walk; but there are several services running through Tideswell (see walk 4), and one of the alternative routes starts from there.

On Friday, Saturday and Sunday there are two buses each way on the Chesterfield – Tideswell – Peak Forest – Manchester route which pass Mount Pleasant Farm, where the minor road north from Wheston joins the A623. This is about half a mile from the route of the walk. They also pass Peak Forest village which you can reach by taking the alternative route up Dam Dale.

Amenities: There are several pubs and cafes in Tideswell, many in Buxton, and the Devonshire Arms at Peak Forest. There are toilets in Tideswell, at the bus shelter in the broad main street (Fountain Square), and at the car parks at Tideswell Dale and the former Miller's Dale station.

The walk follows the road from the tiny village of Wheston, two miles north of Miller's Dale, to a junction near Monksdale House. Here it joins the Limestone Way to traverse Peter Dale and its continuation, Hay Dale (and optionally Dam Dale), before returning to the road north of Wheston.

This is one you can try in the rainy season; it is mostly firm underfoot, though there are a few muddy patches. About half the distance is along very quiet byroads, with a broad grass verge for most of the way. The rest is along paths which form part of the 'Limestone Way' long-distance footpath (Matlock to Castleton). The walk is entirely on limestone. Most of it is fairly level, with one moderately steep descent on a road and a similar ascent on a firm track, so it is easier than many walks of this length.

Although not quite as spectacular as some of the other dry dales, these make an attractive walk and are less rough underfoot than Monk's Dale to the south. They are a good place for wild flowers in spring. The road section of the walk is on a ridge with good views across the dales to the west.

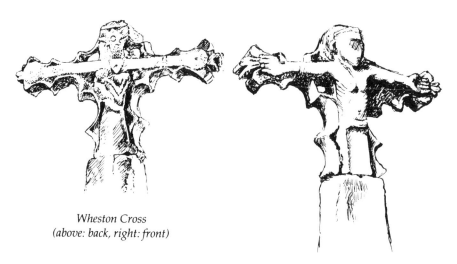

Wheston Cross
(above: back, right: front)

Wheston Cross is a 15th century boundary marker, with a tall shaft surmounted by an ornate cross head with rather primitive images of Christ crucified on one side and the virgin and child on the other. Though much weathered, it is well worth seeing if such things interest you.

This walk is on the 'West' side of the White Peak OS map.

The Walk

Walk southwards along the road to Wheston. This is a tiny village consisting mainly of farms; an imposing one, Wheston Hall, faces you as you reach the village. You may like to make a short diversion to the

3. WHESTON, PETER DALE AND HAY DALE

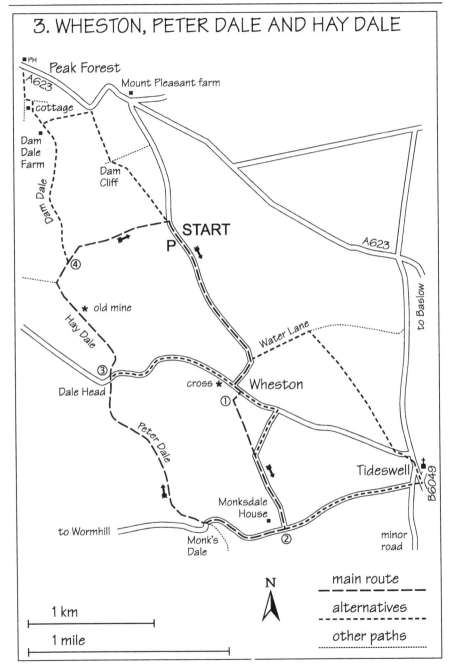

1 km

1 mile

N

main route

alternatives

other paths

right to see Wheston Cross, which stands in a small enclosure on the left of the road just beyond a builder's yard. Otherwise turn left up the village street, then in a few metres turn right up a firm walled track **(1)**. (If this is muddy, go about 300 metres further up the street and turn right at the road junction). Where the track converges with the road, go straight on along it for nearly half a mile till you reach the road junction near Monksdale House **(2)**.

Turn right down the road; this has a little more traffic than the one you have just left, so take care. Where the road bends you can see down into the wooded Monk's Dale on your left. (This same dale is named successively Monk's Dale, Peter Dale, Hay Dale and Dam Dale). Where the road reaches the dale bottom, ignore a gate but go through a squeezer stile to your right a few metres on, with a 'Limestone Way' signpost.

This is Peter Dale, and it is always dry. The dale sides are fairly low, and vary between green slopes and limestone cliffs. After crossing a green field you pass through a short rocky stretch, rough underfoot, and then the dale opens out again. Keep to the bottom of the dale, along another flat green field. The dale sides become vertical cliffs for a while, and then the valley opens out once more as you approach Dale Head, with ruined farm buildings to your left.

Go over a steep step stile (with footpath signpost) to the right of the modern house. Turn right along the road for a few metres, then left over a wooden stile, again signposted 'Limestone Way' **(3)**. This is Hay Dale; the sides are lower than in Peter Dale but there is still some rock in them. Continue up the grassy field at the bottom of the dale. You will come to a mine tip on your right, and behind it at the end of a rock cutting is the entrance to a mine level. It is partly blocked and unsafe to enter, but rusting remains of iron sheets and a mine truck show that it was worked quite recently.

Beyond here the path becomes a pleasant tree-lined avenue, leading to a walled track. Go straight ahead along it. It may be muddy at first but is firm further on. Keep to the track as it swings right out of the dale **(4)**, and climbs to a road. Turn right along this, towards Wheston, to return to your starting point.

Alternative routes

You can reduce the walk to 3 miles, omitting Peter Dale, by turning right instead of left in Wheston. At the dale bottom **(3)** turn right over a wooden stile signposted 'Limestone Way' and you are back on the main route.

Alternatively, park in Wheston or between here and Monksdale house, and follow the walk into and up Peter Dale. When you reach the road at Dale Head, turn right up it to Wheston. This route, which leaves out Hay Dale, is also about 3 miles.

You can extend the walk by about a mile by including Dam Dale. Towards the end of the main walk, after passing the mine and joining the walled track, look out for a step stile on the left where the track bends right and starts to climb **(4)**. Cross it and follow a path between the wall and the dale side for three quarters of a mile. The dale is floored by small green fields.

At Dam Dale Farm the path goes through a wicket gate into a small field. Go over a stile at the far left corner of this and turn right alongside the wall to a gate. Go through this and half left up the hill, aiming for a small quarry on the skyline. Cross a step stile and then a wooden stile, which brings you close to the road and a footpath signpost. Turn right here, over a wooden stile and then another up on the skyline, and follow the wall on your left more gently uphill. After a gateway there are walls both sides and the path reaches the top of a small hill called Dam Cliff. Look back here and admire the view; Peak Forest village down in the valley, Rushup Edge directly in line with the path you have come up, and the shoulder of Kinder Scout in the distance a little further left.

A stile brings you onto a walled track. Go over a step stile almost opposite, slightly to the left, and bear half left across the field but well to the right of the farm. Cross a stile by a waymark post, and make for the far left corner of the field. You will cross a hidden stile with a waymark post, and then a stile at the corner of the field. Go on in the same direction to a gate in the far left corner of the field, where you join the Wheston road at the same point as the main route. Turn half right along the tarmac.

To reach the bus route in Peak Forest village, follow this route up Dam Dale, through the wicket gate and over the stile at Dam Dale farm; but then instead of turning right, bear half left round the hill, towards green farm buildings. Go just to the right of a cottage and over an inconspicuous step stile, then left along a bank which crosses the dale bottom – presumably this is the dam which gave the dale its name, though there is no longer water behind it. Turn right along the tarmac lane, which brings you to the main A623 road opposite the Devonshire Arms. The distance will be much the same as if you had returned to

Mount Pleasant farm. (If you want to reach the route from Peak Forest village instead of Mount Pleasant, turn off the A623 and walk up Damside Lane, almost opposite the Devonshire Arms. Pass the farm and turn left along the bank which crosses the valley, then right over a step stile behind the cottage. Go half left round the hillside to a stile just left of the next farm, but instead of crossing it turn left alongside the wall, go through the next gate and make for a small quarry on the skyline. You are now on the alternative route described above).

You can, if you prefer, start the walk in Tideswell. This will make the distance 5½ miles (or 6 if you include Wheston Cross). See Walk 4 for parking, public transport and amenities in Tideswell. Leave Tideswell along the minor road described in the first alternative to Walk 4. When you pass the Monksdale House road junction and continue towards the dale you are on the route of the main walk.

At the end of the walk after joining the Wheston road, keep on it for nearly a mile – almost to Wheston village. After a bend to the right, when the road starts to drop towards the village, turn left into a straight walled track with overhead wires to the left. This is Water Lane, but in spite of its name it is firm in any weather. (If you want to visit Wheston Cross, follow the road to the village but return to this point). As Water Lane approaches the brow of the hill, turn right into a similar walled track. In about half a mile, Tideswell church comes in sight on the left and the track drops to join a road. Turn left, and take a path to the right of young trees to cut off a bend. Where the road joins another, turn right through the quiet Market Square to the village centre and your starting point.

Walk 4: West of Tideswell

Start: In the centre of Tideswell, in the small free car park (SK151755) on the west side of the broad main street. If this is full it is usually possible to park at the kerbside nearby, or by the church.

Distance: 3½ miles (alternative 4½).

Public transport: Regular bus services (fewer on Sundays) from Chesterfield and Sheffield to Buxton run through the village, and some of these continue to Manchester. There are also some buses from Bakewell. On summer Sundays, a bus timed to give a day out runs from Mansfield and Derby to Tideswell and on to Castleton.

Amenities: There are pubs and cafes in Tideswell, including the Horse and Jockey just south of the car park (unassuming, but good food), the George to the right of the church, and the Anchor north-east of the town at the A623 crossroads. There are also several shops where you can buy the makings of a picnic.

There are public toilets close to the car park, and also at the Tideswell Dale car park a mile south along the main road.

Tideswell church ('The Cathedral of the Peak') is well worth a visit if you are interested in such things. It has some fine brasses, and an attractive modern window installed in 1996.

The walk starts in the large village of Tideswell, with its fine church, and explores the limestone plateau to the west. It uses a part of the 'Limestone Way' long distance footpath. An alternative, rather longer, route takes you down the very quiet and bosky Monk's Dale, but note that this is rocky underfoot and not easy walking.

There are a few muddy patches, so it is best to choose dry weather or a heavy frost.

The walk is mainly on the 'West' side of the OS 'White Peak' map, although Tideswell itself is just over the edge on the 'East' side.

The scale of the sketch map has been enlarged in the neighbourhood of Tideswell, and some detail has been omitted, for clarity.

The Walk

Turn up Sunny Bank Lane, a steep narrow street running west from the north end of the car park. At the top, cross a road and go through the stile opposite. Continue up this field and the next, with the wall on your right, till you meet a walled lane (Slancote Lane) **(1)**. From here you have a good view back over Tideswell with its imposing church.

Turn left along the lane. In less than half a mile, some way beyond a small barn, the lane turns sharp left **(2)**; leave it, going straight ahead through a stile. Aim for a pond by the wall at the bottom of the field, and cross the stile to the left of it. Continue up the field, with the wall on your left, to reach another lane, and turn left along this **(3)**. You are now on the route of the Limestone Way, a long-distance footpath. Before long there is a T junction of lanes and you should take the one on the right, which soon resumes the original direction. This lane may be muddy in places. To your right is Monk's Dale, but because of the lie of the land you cannot see far into it.

In less than half a mile you will come to a gate across the lane. Cross

Tideswell Church

4. WEST OF TIDESWELL

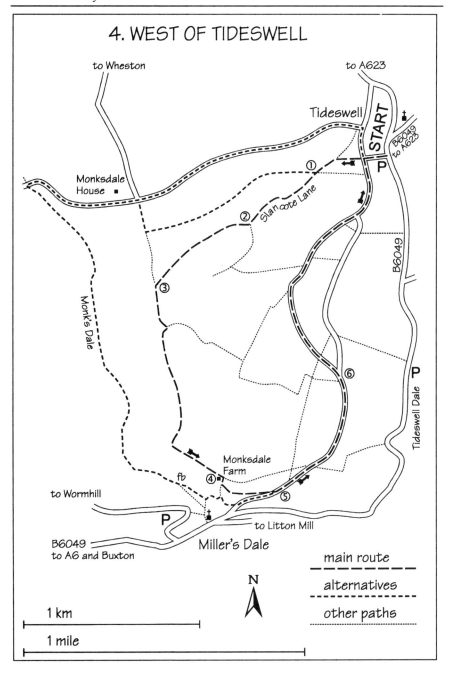

the stile beside it; the lane is muddy for a few metres but soon improves. Continue along the lane, which has now turned a corner so that you can see Millers Dale on the right, with its twin railway viaducts. Go on past a house on the right **(4)** and through a gate. The next gate across the lane, straight ahead, says 'No entry'. In fact only a short stretch of it is private and this is bypassed by stiles on the left, and you can continue across three fields to the road. But this way is little used and is muddy, so it is better to turn right between the two gates, then left through the upper farmyard. Go on along the farm drive to reach a quiet tarmac road **(5)**, and turn left along it.

Where the road forks **(6)** you can go either way – the roads rejoin in half a mile – but the left one is the easier choice because the other drops to a small valley and then climbs again. Where the roads rejoin you will find yourself at Tideswell. Your road runs parallel to the main street, which is below to your right; continue along it till you reach Sunny Bank Lane, and turn down it to return to the car park.

Alternative routes

You will see from the OS map that there are several alternative paths from Tideswell to the track that is used by the Limestone Way, and there is little to choose between them.

You can include the secluded Monk's Dale (a nature reserve) in your walk at the cost of an extra mile, but be warned that the dale is hard walking – the path is obvious, but much of it is over loose rock which can be slippery. The easiest way to reach the dale is to turn right at the top of Sunny Bank Lane and then left along a minor road in 200 metres. Continue for a mile and a quarter, going straight on at the road junction near Monksdale House, to the bottom of Monk's Dale, and follow the path to the left down it.

Alternatively, leave Tideswell as described in the main walk, turning left along the first walled lane (Slancote Lane); but then go right over a stile by a gate in about 150 metres, where the lane levels out. Follow the wall on your right through several squeezers. Where the wall turns right, your next stile is a little to the left and two further stiles bring you to a walled green lane. Go straight across, and across the field opposite, as indicated by a footpath signpost. The next stile is just right of a dewpond. Go up the field, with the wall close on your left, to a step stile leading onto a walled track, and turn right till you reach the road. Turn left to the bottom of Monk's Dale and left down it, as described above.

In wet weather, the last stretch of track before the road may be flooded so the road alternative is to be preferred.

Keep along the bottom of the dale for over a mile until you reach a plank footbridge. Don't cross this, but follow the left side of the dale bottom for a couple of hundred metres, keeping right at a fork, until you find a waymarked footpath climbing the dale side. At a waymark on an old log, climb left to join a track (the Limestone Way) by a narrow gate. Turn right along the track to the road, and turn left along it. In a quarter mile the main route joins this road. (The path up the dale side may be slippery in wet weather. If so, cross the footbridge and take the firmer path sloping up the dale side; after crossing a rocky outcrop it descends beside the church to the main road. Turn left, and immediately fork left up an 'unsuitable for motors' road. The main route joins this a short way up).

Walk 5: Across Chee Dale

Start: Park on the grass verge in Blackwell village (SK125721) at any point between the two bends. Blackwell (no more than a hamlet really) is on a lane running from the A6 trunk road to the B6049 road, which links the A6 to Millers Dale and Tideswell, near to where this road joins the A6. Alternatively use the large car park at the former Millers Dale station (SK138732) just off the B6049, where there are public toilets. This will add rather more than a mile to the walk, unless you use one of the bus services which pass this car park.

Distance: 3 miles (alternatives 3½ to 4, or 6 if combined with walk 17)

Public transport: This walk is well served by buses which run along the A6 only a few hundred metres from the start of the walk; some of them also pass the Millers Dale car park. There is a bus every two hours on the Nottingham-Derby-Buxton-Manchester route, several each day on the Sheffield to Buxton route, and a few buses on the Chesterfield to Buxton route. The Hanley – Sheffield bus passes this way but has limited stops so you will have to change in Buxton or Bakewell. On summer Sundays there are also buses, timed to give you a day out, from Macclesfield and Barnsley. Many of these routes connect with the Manchester to Buxton railway service.

Amenities: The nearest inn is the Anglers Rest in Millers Dale, and there is also a cafe opposite the car park entrance there which is often open at weekends. There are inns and cafes in Tideswell. In the other direction there is the Queens Arms in Taddington village, and also the Waterloo, on the A6, which you pass on the way there. There are of course many opportunities for refreshment in Buxton.

There are public toilets at the Millers Dale car park.

Chee Dale is the narrowest and most spectacular part of the valley of the Wye, which runs through Buxton and down through a series of steep-sided dales until the valley opens out near Ashford. This walk crosses Chee Dale at each end, with fine views into the dale from the high ground on either side; this of course implies a fair amount of uphill walking. It is passable in all weathers, although it can be muddy in places. After heavy rain a scramble may be necessary at Wormhill Springs to avoid a few metres of flooded path. A way round this is described under 'alternative routes'. The short section up Flag Dale is

Chee Dale from Mosley Farm Path

not shown on the map as a right of way, and I do not know whether the owner approves of walkers, but it is well used and unobstructed; you can easily avoid it if you wish. The only road walking is a quarter mile of very quiet lane at Blackwell.

This walk can be combined with walk 17 to make a six mile route, starting either at Chelmorton as described there or at Blackwell as described here.

The little village of Wormhill, which you touch if you take the alternative route avoiding Wormhill Springs, is one of those which has a well-dressing in summer: it is less crowded than most of these. For the date, consult the Peak Park's yearly broadsheet or your local tourist information centre.

This walk is on the 'West' side of the White Peak map.

The Walk

Walk to the bend at the east end of the village and take the drive to Blackwell Hall farm. Follow the lane where it bears right between two groups of buildings, straight on down the hill for a few hundred metres,

5. ACROSS CHEE DALE

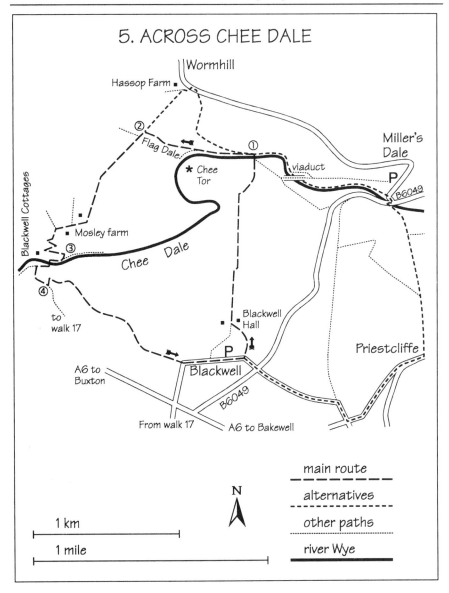

and on round a right-hand bend into a field. Here turn left and walk down the field alongside the wall. Where the wall turns off to the left, go straight on and over a stile. Go on to an obvious gateway, with a spectacular view down into Chee Dale on your left. The former railway line in the dale was the Midland main line from London via Derby to Manchester. It was closed in the 1960s and much of it now forms a footpath called the Monsal Trail, although there are several deviations in this area where tunnels have been sealed.

Beyond the gateway the path bears to the right and zigzags down the steep hillside into Chee Dale to a footbridge over the Wye **(1)**. Cross it and turn left along the riverside path. (If you use the Millers Dale car park, return to it by turning right just before the bridge and taking a path which climbs gently to a gate leading onto the Monsal Trail. Turn left along it, over the viaduct, and you will reach the car park in about half a mile. At the start of the walk, walk west from the car park along the trail to the viaduct; but instead of crossing it, take a steep path on the right which descends to the riverside path. Turn right along it, and at the footbridge go straight on instead of crossing. If the riverside path is very muddy you may prefer to go over the viaduct and take the path on the right, just before the tunnel mouth, to the footbridge: cross it and turn left).

Ignore a path which slopes up the hillside (unless you want to avoid the possible problems described below) and continue alongside the river. In about a quarter of a mile there is a side valley on the right, and you cross a side stream: this is Wormhill Springs. There are a few metres here which can be tricky if the river is very high, but they can be managed with care (see 'alternative routes' to avoid this difficulty and the path up Flag Dale). Go over the stile. Our path now bears right up the dry Flag Dale, but you may like to deviate for a few metres along the main path to see the imposing cliff of Chee Tor on the opposite side of the river: it is best seen when the leaves are off the trees.

The short path up Flag Dale is not shown as a right of way, but it is well used and does not cross any walls or fences. The dale is narrow and rocky underfoot, and well wooded. Where the vegetation opens out you will find a cross path (a right of way) descending one side of the dale and climbing the other **(2)**. The path that continues ahead is not a right of way. Take the path on the left which zigzags up the hillside, passing beds of wild pansies in the spring.

Cross the stile at the top, then up the field with the wall a short distance on your left to the next stile. Cross this and continue in the same general direction over another stile (or a gap in the wall) to reach a metalled farm lane. Turn left along it, and continue along the lane as it turns right through a group of farm buildings at Mosley Farm. Beyond them a metalled road (now a cul-de-sac) leads off to the right; but you should turn left on a green track which zigzags down the steep hillside, with fine views of the upper part of Chee Dale. This part of the dale is not wooded, so the limestone crags can be seen well. At the junction that you see on the old railway, the main line swung north into Great Rocks Dale, now a vast quarry, and on through a tunnel to Manchester; a branch line ran west beside the Wye to end at Buxton.

The path takes you under the old main line and joins the riverside path (3). Turn right along it, to Blackwell Cottages, and cross the footbridge. Then turn left off the track, passing to the left of a shed, across the disused Buxton branch of the railway by the bridge or a pair of stiles, and up a side dale – a nature reserve with a fine display of cowslips and orchids in spring.

If you are combining this with walk 17 continue up this valley to the road, but for the main route cross a stile on the left (4) and follow the path which climbs steeply onto a ridge between the dales, turning right along the crest of the ridge. Where it levels out, bear left and cross a stile on the right (after admiring the fine view into Chee Dale from the dale rim on your left). Turn left to another stile, then right alongside the wall to a gravel track. Turn left along this for a few metres and cross a stile on the right; then bear to the left, climbing only slightly, till you find yourself alongside a ruined wall. This leads you to a gate. Go over the stile beside it, and along the walled track. In a quarter of a mile this brings you to the road in Blackwell village; go straight ahead along it to return to your car.

Alternative routes

If the river is very high and you cannot cross the side stream at Wormhill Springs, or if you have qualms about walking up Flag Dale, there is an alternative route which adds about half a mile. After crossing the footbridge (1), instead of following the riverside path to Flag Dale take the one which slopes up the valley side. This will bring you out on the road by a cottage at the bottom of Wormhill village. (If you start from Millers Dale you can walk there directly along the quiet road). Turn left up the road, then immediately left again onto a track through Hassop Farm. Beyond the buildings bear left from the track, diagonally across three fields with obvious stiles, and down into Flag Dale where you meet the main route. Continue up the opposite side of the dale as described above.

If you prefer (and especially if you have parked at Millers Dale) you can take an alternative route back to Blackwell. This is slightly longer, about 3½ miles (whether you park at Blackwell or Miller's Dale); it does not climb to the north of Chee Dale so there is less up and down, although the up is quite steep. The track just before Priestcliffe village can be very muddy in wet weather. A short part of the way is shared with walk 6, so you could combine the two.

Follow the route as described to the footbridge **(1)**, but turn right instead of left along Chee Dale. Continue under the viaduct (unless you parked at Miller's Dale, in which case go up the path to the viaduct and turn left along the Monsal Trail). Go on along the dale to a minor road and turn right (if you parked at Miller's Dale, return to the car park entrance and turn right down the road under the bridge). At the main road turn right, then immediately beyond the bridge turn sharp left into a path which climbs steeply up the dale side, with steps in places. Ignore a level path on the left (walk 6 would bring you out here), unless you wish to walk a few metres along it to a seat with a good view across the dale.

Go through a stile at the top of the slope. Continue straight ahead, through a gateway under a tree and two more gateways, to a walled track, and follow this to Priestcliffe village. Turn right along the road (walk 6 turns left instead), taking the upper road at the fork, and turn right at the crossroads. At the next crossroads go straight on to return to Blackwell and your car.

The path along Chee Dale itself is one of the finest walks in the White Peak, part of it being on stepping stones in the river under overhanging rocks. It is impassable when the river is high. This is a popular route forming part of the Monsal Trail and you will find it described in several guide books, so I shall not repeat it here.

Walk 6: Miller's Dale and Priestcliffe

Start: The Miller's Dale station car park (SK138733). There are toilets here, and
                        at weekends the local weather forecast is usually displayed in the window
                        of the ranger's office on the station platform.

Distance: 3¾ miles (alternatives 2½ to 4)

Public transport: About six buses a day (three on Sunday) on the Sheffield – Tideswell –
                        Buxton route, and three a day (none on Sunday) on the Chesterfield –
                        Tideswell Buxton route, stop on the main road below Millers Dale station.
                        On summer Sundays there are rambler's buses on the Mansfield – Derby
                        – Castleton route, and occasionally on the Barnsley – Castleton – Buxton
                        route, which also pass this way.

                        The Nottingham – Derby – Manchester route (about 6 a day) and Hanley
                        – Buxton – Sheffield route (about 4 a day) pass through Taddington; this
                        is rather more than half a mile from Priestcliffe. Alight by the cafe at the
                        top of Taddington village. (The Waterloo Hotel is a quarter of a mile further
                        on, at SK1323714, but gives you somewhere warm to wait for your return
                        bus).

Amenities: The Waterloo Hotel on the A6 south of Miller's Dale, the Queens Head
                        in Taddington, the Anglers Rest in Miller's Dale and the Church Inn in
                        Chelmorton all serve hot food. There is a cafe opposite the Miller's Dale
                        car park entrance which is usually open at summer weekends, and also
                        a cafe at Taddington where the village street joins the A6. There are also
                        cafes and pubs in Tideswell.

                        There are toilets at the Miller's Dale station car park.

This walk starts at the former Miller's Dale station (SK138733), crosses
the valley, and follows a concessionary path through a nature reserve
before joining the footpath to Priestcliffe. From here it takes a track
towards Brushfield and descends to Miller's Dale near Litton Mill,
returning by the Monsal Trail.

The Monsal trail follows part of the route of the former Midland
Railway main line, which ran from London St. Pancras via Derby to
Manchester. Miller's Dale station was the junction for the Buxton
branch and also a popular tourist destination, with five platforms. The
line north of Matlock was closed when the West Coast route was
electrified in the 1960s, and this part of it is now an all weather footpath.

Miller's Dale – Old Station

Several tunnels are closed and bypassed by rougher paths; so this trail is little used by cyclists and horses, although they are permitted.

The walk is entirely on limestone. Although most of it is firm, there are stretches which may be muddy. The descent into Miller's Dale will be slippery if there is snow on the ground. The view is best when the leaves are off the trees, and the flowers are at their best in spring.

Miller's Dale was seriously disfigured by large quarries and active lime kilns until a few decades ago. These have been dismantled, and nature is rapidly reclaiming the dale side – with some help from the Peak Park authorities. Much of this side of the dale is now a nature reserve, and all of the paths pass through it.

Most of this walk is on the 'west' side of the 'White Peak' OS map, although that map does not show the concessionary paths. Litton Mill is just on the 'East' side of the sheet.

My sketch map is drawn with East at the top.

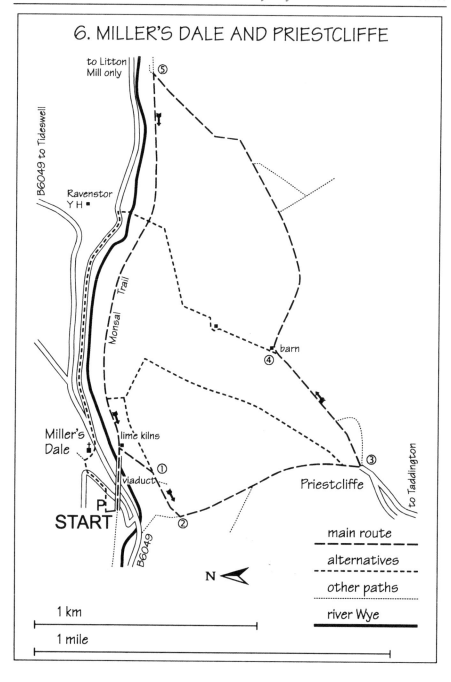

6. MILLER'S DALE AND PRIESTCLIFFE

The Walk

Go through the iron gate to the left of the station buildings and turn left over whichever of the two viaducts is open. Immediately beyond it, turn right up the steps signposted 'Lime kilns'. This brings you to the foot of a large bank of disused lime kilns, and a further set of steps on the right takes you to the top of the kilns. Walk along the top of the kilns if you like, to inspect them and admire the view, but return to the top of the steps and take the path into the wood, past a Nature Reserve information board.

The concessionary path slopes up the hillside. This is the route of a railway which brought limestone down from the quarries to the top of the lime kilns. It meets a level path (1), formerly a rail track linking several quarries. You can see traces of the brake gear which controlled trucks on the incline, and the depressions left by the sleepers, as well as ruins of quarry buildings. Turn right along this path. Soon the former railway turns left into an old quarry, but your route carries straight on to a seat at a gap in the trees. From here you have a fine view across Miller's Dale, with the station below you and Monk's Dale branching off opposite. You can just see the chimney of the vast limeworks and quarries in Great Rocks Dale over the trees to your left.

Beyond the seat the path bears left, and soon meets an older footpath coming steeply up the hill (2). Turn left along it, up a few steps and on steeply till you reach a stile at the top. Go straight on, over a stile by a gateway under a tree and then two more gateways to a walled track, and go forward along it. This track may be muddy, although you can avoid the worst of it; on my last visit it was clogged by drifted snow.

In less than half a mile the track brings you to the road end at the hamlet of Priestcliffe, by a seat and a forest of signs (3). Turn left along a firm walled track, passing left of a cottage, and continue till the track forks in front of a barn (4). A shorter way goes straight on, but the main route turns right and continues up the hill, passing traces of mining as it levels out. Here you leave the track, which turns sharp right towards Brushfield, and go straight ahead through a stile. By it is a sign telling you that you are entering another Derbyshire Wildlife Trust reserve.

The path leads through a very long narrow field, with depressions left by mining. At the end, bear left and follow the yellow waymarks over a stile, then to the left alongside the wall down to a wooden stile beside a gate. From here a clear path bears slightly right between hawthorn bushes, and steeply down towards a row of cottages by Litton Mill.

When you reach a bridge over the former railway (5), do not cross it but go down the steps on your right. Then turn left along the Monsal Trail. This will bring you back to the car park in rather less than a mile and a half. At first the way is through a steep rocky cutting, but beyond this the trail is cut along the hillside with the river Wye below you. At a gap in the trees you can see the red roofs of Ravenstor youth hostel on the hillside opposite, above a limestone cliff. Beyond more cuttings, masonry and concrete slabs on the left are the remains of massive quarry buildings which were demolished twenty or thirty years ago and are now almost hidden by trees. Just beyond them is the preserved bank of lime kilns you saw at the start of the walk, and the car park is a few metres further on.

Alternative routes

For a rather shorter walk (about 2½ miles), follow the main route past Priestcliffe but go straight on at the barn (4) instead of forking right. The track leads to a house. Go left over a stile just before the gate and then follow the wall round to the right, and admire the spectacular view over Miller's dale. The second of two footpath signposts indicates the path sloping down the dale side, more or less towards the red roof of Ravenstor Youth hostel which you can see on the far side of the dale.

The path is a bit vague at first, with occasional yellow posts to mark the way, but becomes clear later. Beyond a stile it enters a wood and continues downhill, with steps on the steepest stretches, until another stile brings you out on the Monsal Trail. Turn left to reach the car park in rather less than a mile; or to see more of the river and the spectacular cliffs of the dale, and pass the Anglers Rest, go straight ahead down a path waymarked 'Ravenstor'. Cross the footbridge, and walk left along the very quiet road. Where it joins the main road, turn right up a footpath to the left of the church; keep alongside the wall on your left after the kissing gate, and at the road turn left for a few metres to the car park entrance.

Botanists may like to start the walk by walking on along the trail past the limekilns, instead of going up the steps to them, and taking a signposted footpath on the right about 300 metres on. The path slopes up the hillside to the level of the quarry floor. You should not enter the quarry, but in season you will see a wealth of lime-loving plants over the fence. From here you have a choice: either way will add about a quarter of a mile to the distance given for the main walk. The second choice is a bit less steep than the main route and avoids the worst muddy patch. The first choice is the level concessionary path to the right; this meanders pleasantly past the old quarries to come out, in about a quarter of a mile, at the top of the incline above the lime kilns on the main route. Second choice is the very clear path on up the hillside, round the edge of the quarry. At the top, a faint path over a series of stiles leads you across the fields. For most of the way you walk alongside a wall, crossing from side to side of it at intervals. Beyond a small valley, the path crosses to the right of the wall again and veers to the right through more stiles. The last one, as you approach Priestcliffe village, is a little further to the right by a footpath signpost. Turn left along the walled track; you are now back on the main route – beyond the muddiest part of it – and soon reach point **(3)**.

Walk 7: Water-cum-Jolly Dale

Start: At the cemetery (SK163742) on the minor road from Litton village to Monsal head via Cressbrook. There is room for several cars on the verge opposite the cemetery entrance. For one of the alternative routes you should use instead the Tideswell Dale car park (SK154742), though this may be full on summer Sundays: there is a small charge.

Distance: 4 miles (alternatives 3 to 5 miles).

Public transport: Two buses a day (not Sunday) on the Bakewell to Tideswell route pass Cressbrook Mill and the cemetery on their way to Litton.

There are several buses a day (fewer on Sunday) on the Sheffield to Buxton, Chesterfield to Buxton and Bakewell to Tideswell routes which pass through Litton Village, half a mile from the main route, and also pass the Tideswell Dale car park on the alternative route. On certain days there are Chesterfield to Manchester buses passing these places, and on summer Sundays also a single bus from Rochdale and Oldham going on to Matlock.

Amenities: There are pubs and cafes in Tideswell and at Monsal Head, and also the Anglers Rest at Miller's Dale. A cafe opposite the Miller's Dale station car park (SK139733) is sometimes open at weekends. The Red Lion at Litton is more of a restaurant than a pub and may not be open at lunchtime. If the developments at Cressbrook and Litton mills go ahead there may be opportunities for refreshment there.

There are picnic tables at the Tideswell Dale car park.

There are toilets at the Tideswell Dale car park; also in Tideswell and at the Miller's Dale station car park.

The walk starts on the plateau south-east of Tideswell, drops to Litton Mill and follows Water-cum-Jolly Dale to Cressbrook Mill, then climbs through Cressbrook village and along the edge of Cressbrook Dale to return to the start.

Water-cum-Jolly Dale is one of the most attractive short dales in the Peak District. Not named on many maps, it is the section of the Wye Valley between Litton and Cressbrook mills, thus linking Miller's Dale and Monsal Dale. The concessionary path along it is long established and widely used. It forms part of the Monsal Trail, as it by-passes a section of the old railway where the tunnels are closed.

Cressbrook Mill

The contrasting mills at Litton and Cressbrook were both built for textile manufacture. Cressbrook Mill is an attractive pedimented building, Litton Mill a rather ugly huddle of buildings. Both have been disused for many years, but Litton Mill is being converted in 1996 to a leisure complex. Cressbrook Mill, although some essential repairs have been done, is rapidly becoming derelict because the owners and the planning authorities cannot agree on its future.

This walk is best done in the off-season, since much of Water-cum-Jolly Dale and Cressbrook Dale is screened by trees when they are in leaf. It is entirely on limestone.

About half a mile of the main walk is along quiet roads. Some of the remaining sections may be muddy after heavy rain; one of the alternative routes avoids the worst section. In very wet weather the path through Water-cum-Jolly Dale may be flooded and the walk is then impracticable.

The Walk

From the cemetery walk south (away from Litton) along the road for a quarter of a mile. Beyond a tall row of houses take the road on the right, signposted 'Littonslack'. Where the road turns sharp right in another quarter of a mile **(1)**, go straight ahead over a stile beside an iron gate. You can take the track which runs down the bottom of the little valley, but for a better view take the one on its left which runs towards a chimney (a flue ran up the hillside to it from the mill below), and then curves right to descend to the first track. You can see only a little of the rocky side of Water-cum-Jolly dale to the left, but there is a good view up Miller's Dale on your right; the prominent red-roofed house is Ravenstor youth hostel.

A short way past a gate and stile the track joins a tarmac road. Follow it down to the massive gateposts of Litton Mill **(2)** and turn left through them. The concessionary path (a firm track, though sometimes muddy in places) runs through the mill yard, then turns right over the mill tailrace and left into Water-cum-Jolly Dale. It runs between the river Wye and the mill tailrace, which is well below river level at this point. The path crosses the tailrace again where it joins the river. From here the dale becomes more spectacular, with high limestone cliffs, though these are partly hidden when the trees are in leaf.

By a small weir are the remains of a waterwheel which used to pump water to Cressbrook Hall high above. The wall is a convenient resting place. The old railway makes a brief appearance between tunnels high on the opposite side of the dale. On your left is a shaft of rock completely detached from the cliff, though you will only see it when the trees are bare. The stream broadens to become the millpond for Cressbrook Mill. The path runs below overhanging waterworn cliffs, and houses built originally for mill workers can be seen above. A wooden bridge crosses the mill leat. Do not turn right (with the Monsal Trail) across the river but go ahead past a stone yard, a building with pointed windows which may be open for refreshments, and the derelict Cressbrook Mill – the mill may be restored if planning permission is granted.

Beyond the mill you reach the road **(3)** and turn left along it into the wooded Cressbrook Dale. The most direct and least steep way is by the right fork; but a quieter and more interesting road is the one which forks left and left again, passing houses and the little school. Half way up the hill, behind an iron shed, is a roadside memorial seat. At the top of the hill, below a terrace of houses which forms part of Cressbrook village, you come to a road junction. Turn right, opposite the lodge of Cress-brook Hall. At the next junction turn right again and walk gently downhill.

Where the road doubles back on itself **(4)**, towards Cressbrook Mill –

7. WATER-CUM-JOLLY DALE

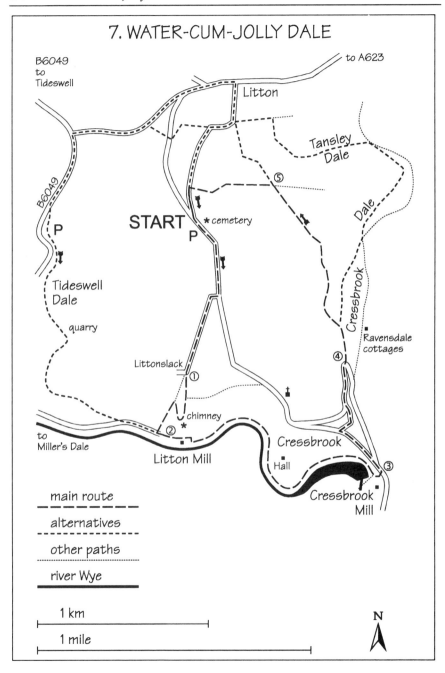

B6049
to
Tideswell

to A623

Litton

Tansley
Dale

B6049

P

START P   * cemetery

⑤

Dale

Cressbrook

Tideswell
Dale

quarry

Littonslack

①

chimney

② *

to
Miller's Dale

Litton Mill

Ravensdale
cottages

④

Cressbrook
Hall

③

Cressbrook
Mill

main route

alternatives

other paths

river Wye

1 km

1 mile

N

you will have come up this way if you took the right fork – go straight ahead on a firm track. This runs through a wood for two or three hundred metres. Just before it leaves the wood, take a clear footpath on the left. It climbs steeply up the dale side, but steps make it firm underfoot. At the top the path turns to the right along the rim of the dale. This section can be slippery when wet, though not dangerous. There are occasional glimpses through the trees of the rocky far side of the dale.

Eventually Litton village comes into sight. The path goes through a wooden squeezer on your left and heads towards the village, crossing the next wall by a stone squeezer. Continue in the same direction diagonally across the field, past a line of mounds left by old mine diggings, to a wall gap in the far corner. Now bear slightly more to the left, towards a prominent building at the left end of the village, and over three step stiles (the second is ruinous but there is a gateway near it). The third stile brings you to a walled track **(5)**. If you want to visit Litton (or your bus is there) go straight across, then half left. Cross a stile in the wall on your left and continue in the same direction to the valley bottom. Go through a stile in the wall which runs along the bottom of the valley, onto a path which leads straight up a narrow field. This brings you to the road into the village (turn left along this road for the cemetery). But the main route is left along the track, which may be muddy after wet weather. At the road, turn left and you will be back at the cemetery in a few hundred metres.

Alternative routes

If you start at the Tideswell Dale car park (SK154742) on the B6049, less than a mile south of Tideswell village, you can include the pleasant Tideswell Dale at the cost of increasing the distance to 4½ miles. From the far end of the car park, near the toilet block, follow the path down the dale for nearly a mile until it reaches a road. (Those interested in geology may like to make a short diversion via the old quarry on the left – steps at the far end of the quarry floor lead back to the dale bottom). Turn left along the road, past a row of cottages, to the gates of Litton Mill **(2)** and follow the main route from there.

After climbing out of Cressbrook Dale, you can continue into Litton and look round the attractive village before turning left down the road, and left again when you reach the bottom of the dale, to return to the Tideswell Dale car park. There is a footway beside the road. If you do not want to go into the village you can save a few hundred metres by turning left when you reach the metalled road on the outskirts of the village. Where the road turns left, go straight ahead across several small fields with the wall on your right. At the last field before the lane, go diagonally left to a stile giving onto the lane. Go straight across, and steeply down the field to a stile just left of a house. Turn left along the road, and left at the junction, to return to the car park.

A further diversion, to include Tansley Dale, adds another half mile. After climbing through Cressbrook village and taking the track through the wood **(4)**, go straight ahead instead of turning up the path on the left. Shortly follow a path sloping down to the bottom of Cressbrook Dale. From here the right of way slopes up the valley side to the right, and then steeply down again (see walk 2); but although this way gives the better view, the path along the dale bottom is an accepted route and less strenuous. Where Tansley dale enters on the left, go into it and follow the obvious path up the dale, climbing steeply to the right at the head of it, to a walled lane. Turn left along the lane. It reaches a metalled road. Turn right for the village; or go straight ahead, then over a stile where the road turns left, as described above.

After heavy rain the path above Cressbrook Dale, and the track leading back to the cemetery, will be muddy. You can avoid this, and shorten the route by a mile, by continuing up the road through Cressbrook village instead of turning right opposite the lodge of Cressbrook Hall. Go straight on where another road joins from the right, watching out for traffic, and on past the church to reach the cemetery in about a mile. For Litton village take the right fork; for the Tideswell Dale car park fork left, and look out for a pair of stiles in about a quarter of a mile. Take the one on the left, go steeply down the field, and turn left along the road and left again at the road junction.

Walk 8: Monsal Head and Hay Dale

Start: At the large public car park behind the Monsal Head Hotel (SK 185715), entered from the B6465 Ashford to Wardlow road. There is a charge for parking. The small car park in front of the hotel is for short stays only. There are a few places in the upper part of Hay Dale where a car can be parked safely on the verge, and there is a small car park at Upperdale just west of the crossroads although this may be full at summer weekends. Parking on the Little Longstone road near Monsal Head is discouraged because it obstructs the traffic, and there are parking restrictions on some other roads in the area in summer.

Distance: 4 miles (alternative 5 miles).

Public transport: On weekdays there are buses about every two hours between Bakewell and Tideswell via Monsal Head, some of them continuing to Castleton via Hope Station where they connect with the Manchester to Sheffield local trains. There are also a few Bakewell to Monsal Head local buses (not on Saturday afternoon). On Sundays, in summer only, there are four buses each way between Bakewell and Castleton via Tideswell and Hope station.

Amenities: The Monsal Head Hotel and adjacent restaurants and tea rooms offer a wide choice of refreshments. The Packhorse Inn at Little Longstone, on the route, offers food although it struck me as a little expensive: likewise the Bull's Head at Wardlow. There is also the White Lion in Great Longstone, and there are more inns and cafes in Ashford and Bakewell.

There are public toilets at the Monsal Head car park.

This walk starts at Monsal Head and descends to the Monsal Trail. It then follows a quiet by-road up Hay Dale, crosses the fields to Little Longstone, and returns for a short way alongside the road. (This Hay Dale should not be confused with another the other side of Tideswell, included in Walk 3).

The view from Monsal Head is one of the most famous in the Peak district. Hay Dale is dry, rocky at first but wooded later. There are more good views from the later part of the walk.

Just over a mile of this walk is along a quiet by-road. Another half-mile is along other roads, where there is an adequate footway or grass verge. The walk is satisfactory after rain, except that the first

Monsal Head Viaduct in Steam Days

stretch – the steep path from Monsal Head to the Monsal Trail – may be slippery. This can be avoided by following the road down to Upperdale.

The Walk

Make your way by any of several short paths from the car park to the minor road which leaves the B6465 and passes in front of the hotel. From here there is a magnificent view in both directions along Monsal Dale (a part of the valley of the Wye), which makes a sharp bend at this point. Below you is a viaduct on what used to be the Midland Railway main line from Manchester to London. When the line was built in 1861 it aroused much opposition – John Ruskin, the art critic, growled that 'The valley is gone and the Gods with it, and now every fool in Buxton can be at Bakewell in half an hour, and every fool in Bakewell in Buxton'. But the viaduct is now so much a part of the landscape that there would be just as much uproar if it was removed. The railway closed in 1965, when electrification of the alternative route to Manchester was complete, and the route now forms the 'Monsal Trail'. This is open to cyclists and horses as well as walkers; but because there are

8. MONSAL HEAD AND HAY DALE

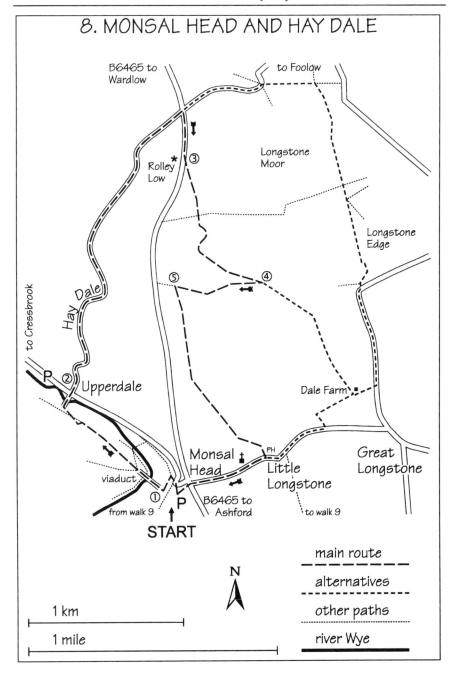

B6465 to Wardlow

to Foolow

Longstone Moor

Rolley* Low

③

Longstone Edge

⑤   ④

to Cressbrook

Hay Dale

P ② Upperdale

Dale Farm

Monsal Head

PH

Little Longstone

Great Longstone

viaduct

① P B6465 to Ashford

from walk 9

to walk 9

START

N

1 km

1 mile

main route

alternatives

other paths

river Wye

several closed tunnels which are bypassed by narrower paths, walkers have much of it to themselves. There are plans to re-open a steam railway along this route between Matlock and Buxton, and the line has already reached Rowsley, but it will be many years before it gets as far as here.

Where the road bends sharply to the right there are several gaps in the wall; take the wide one and turn right down a steep stony footpath. In fifty metres or so, turn left along a similar path signposted to the viaduct. At the bottom you will reach the Monsal Trail (1). To your left is a blocked tunnel; your way is to the right, across the viaduct and through a rocky cutting, where you will find many lime-loving plants and a few fossils in the rock.

Beyond a brick overbridge is the site of Monsal Dale station, where an ugly brick building has been made into a shelter. Go to the left of this, down to a lane, and follow this to the right under the railway and across the river to Upperdale, a hamlet of only three or four houses. At the crossroads (2) go straight ahead, up the road which runs the length of the dry Hay Dale. The road is narrow and winding, but there is usually little traffic.

The way is steep at first, and the dale sides rocky; but soon the slope eases and the road runs through woodland and then open grassland, with obvious signs of old lead mining on the right. Keep your eyes on the roadside walls, especially on the left beyond this point, as there are some fine samples of fossil plant stems built into them.

After rather more than a mile you reach a crossroads. Turn right; there is more traffic on this road, but there is an adequate grass verge. On the skyline, immediately to the right of the road, you can see a low mound with a broken wall along the top. This is Rolley Low, a prehistoric burial mound. Just before you reach it there is an inconspicuous squeezer stile on the left, its three stone slabs full of fossils (3). Go through this stile, and over a wooden stile in a wire fence just beyond it. Now continue in almost the same direction, just slightly more to the right, along the contour (there is a faint path). Cross first an inconspicuous step stile, then a squeezer which can easily be seen on the skyline, and then a wooden stile (with a redundant squeezer close to it) beside an iron gate.

Continue ahead – there is no obvious path – leaving a concrete dewpond to your right and aiming between two plantations. As you come level with the first of these you will find a concrete step-stile on your left. Cross it, and walk to the right between the fence and wall. Curve left with the fence, along an obvious green track, and keep right at the fork where the fence goes left. From here there is a good view over Great Longstone; Bakewell is hidden by the low hill beyond. The track brings you to two stiles beside iron gates, one after the other, and onto a firm walled lane **(4)**.

Turn right along the lane, which passes a plantation on the left and then another on the right. About a hundred metres beyond this, and a similar distance short of the road, cross a double stile with a footpath sign on your left **(5)**. Head slightly left across the field, to the left of an isolated tree, and you will come to a stile at the left end of a wall. Cross this and walk down the field, keeping close to the wall on your left and crossing a couple of stiles, till you reach a corner with no stile; go a short way right, towards a farm building, and cross the stile on your left.

Now bear slightly left down the field, ignoring the track which goes sharp left and leaving a small concrete pond to your right, to cross a stile (with a footpath sign) in a wall corner near a large ash tree. The valley leads down to an iron gate, but your way is over an inconspicuous step stile some metres to the right of it. Follow the wall on your right until there is a step stile in it; go over this, and continue with the wall now on your left until you find an iron gate facing you. Go through it; the path squeezes just left of a farm building and down a short drive to reach the road at a footpath sign. You are now in Little Longstone village.

The Packhorse Inn is immediately to your left, but your route is to the right along the road (there is a footway alongside), past the picturesque little Congregational church, to return to Monsal Head in about a third of a mile.

Alternative routes

You will add only a little to your route (but another quarter mile of road walking) if, after passing the two iron gates and reaching the walled track **(4)**, you turn left instead of right along it and follow it down to Dale Farm. The track turns sharply left at the farm, but you should instead go over a wooden stile on the right and follow the wall on your left, crossing a step stile. Pass between a house on the left and a ruined building, then go over a step stile by a gate on your left into a walled green lane. You will shortly reach the road. Turn right along it, through Little Longstone and back to Monsal Head.

To add about a mile, when you reach the crossroads at the top of Hay Dale go straight ahead towards Foolow. In a quarter of a mile at a sharp lefthand bend, cross a stile on the right (with a footpath signpost) and walk up the field alongside the wall on your left, through an extensively mined area and across a ruined cross wall. Take care if you stray from the path, as there may be open or indequately capped shafts. Where the slope eases there is a step stile between wooden posts on your left. Do not cross it, but turn right along a visible path. This winds up through the heather to the top of the ridge, where you will find a signpost.

Go straight on downhill, to a path junction on a raised bank, and continue straight ahead alongside traces of an old wall. Soon this is replaced by a narrow cutting which ends in a spoil heap at the highest point, relics of old mining. From this point there is a fine view. The path continues to a gate and stile in a wire fence. Cross the stile: the path now goes left for a few metres and then steeply downhill through trees to meet a road. Turn right along this and walk carefully (it is quiet but narrow) for nearly half a mile to the outskirts of Great Longstone, and turn right into a narrow tarmac lane with a 'Dale Farm' sign. (If you miss this turning, just turn right at the road junction). Where the lane turns sharp right behind Dale Farm, go straight ahead over a wooden stile and follow the instructions for the first alternative route.

Walk 9: Ashford and Fin Cop

Start: At the car park at the west end of Ashford village (SK194698), reached
                        by a short lane from the roundabout. This car park is small and may be
                        full at weekends. There is sometimes an overflow park in the adjacent
                        field; if not, it is usually possible to park at the kerbside at this end of the
                        village.

                        Alternatively, use the large public car park at Monsal Head (SK185715);
                        there is a charge for parking.

Distance: 3½ miles (alternative 4¾), plus an extra mile if you obtain permission to
                        visit the highest point of Fin Cop.

Public transport: See walks 10 (for Ashford) and 8 (for Monsal Head).

Amenities: There are several pubs and cafes in Ashford. The Monsal Head Hotel
                        and adjacent cafe offer a choice of refreshments, and the Packhorse Inn
                        at Little Longstone offers food although its prices are above average.
                        There are picnic tables at the Monsal Head car park.

                        There are toilets at both the Ashford and Monsal Head car parks.

The walk starts at Ashford village and ascends the gentle slopes behind
Fin Cop, with a fine view where it reaches the rim of Monsal Dale. There
is a branch path to the summit of Fin Cop, but this is not a right of way
and you should obtain permission beforehand from the Chatsworth
Estate Office (01246-582204 or 01246-582242) if you want to use it. The

Sheepwash Bridge, Ashford

walk descends to Monsal Head and Little Longstone, and returns across the fields to Ashford.

About three quarters of a mile is along quiet roads, and for half this distance there is a footway alongside the road. A few parts of the route are muddy after rain, but if you wear boots you should have no difficulty.

The sketch map is drawn with East at the top; the scale is distorted at Ashford to show the route more clearly.

The Walk

From the car park walk along the short access road to the village street at the west end of the village (where there is a seat and shelter in the middle of a roundabout) and turn right up Vicarage Lane. In about 50 metres take a footpath on the left which leads steeply up, past houses, to a stile. Go straight ahead across a large field, aiming for a pair of trees on the skyline, and cross the stile beyond them into a walled track **(1)**. (The OS map shows the right of way as bearing slightly left and joining the lane further on, but the stile described seems to be the preferred way). This track has the delightful name of Pennyunk lane, according to the latest OS map.

Turn left along the track, past a barn and a bungalow, and follow it gently uphill round several corners. Where it ends, at a gate and stile, go straight up the field with the wall on your left to another gate and stile. Beyond the stile turn right, past a dewpond, and the path becomes a walled lane again. In less than half a mile this brings you to the rim of Monsal Dale **(2)**, with a magnificent view – more impressive than the famous one from Monsal Head because you are higher. The dale bends sharply below you, and the viaduct on the old railway – now the Monsal Trail footpath – can be seen below to your right.

A path to the left along the dale edge leads in half a mile to the highest point of Fin Cop, with fine views into the dale. However this is not a right of way and you should only use it if you have permission (see above). It is close to a steep slope so children must be kept under control. If you do explore it, return to this point as it does not form a through route.

Continue along the dale edge, dropping slightly, to reach the road at Monsal Head; besides the hotel and cafe, there are picnic tables here and often an ice cream van, and there are public toilets behind the hotel.

9. ASHFORD AND FIN COP

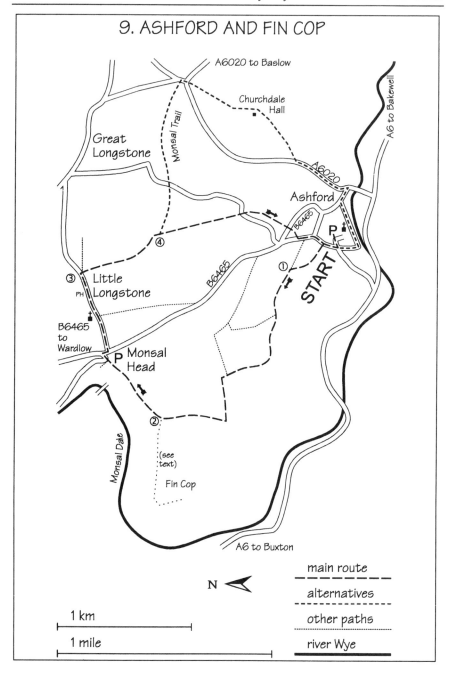

A6020 to Baslow

Churchdale Hall

Monsal Trail

A6 to Bakewell

Great Longstone

A6020

Ashford

B6465

P

① START

③ Little Longstone
PH

B6465 to Wardlow

P Monsal Head

B6465

②

(see text)

Monsal Dale

Fin Cop

A6 to Buxton

N

main route
alternatives
other paths
river Wye

1 km

1 mile

Pass the hotel, cross the main road and take the road opposite to Little Longstone – there is a footway alongside. You will pass the attractive Congregational church, and the Packhorse Inn; then at the bottom of the dip and just beyond a large house on the left **(3)** you will see an array of three gates and two stiles on your right, all leading into the same field. Cross either stile and bear right down the valley; keep a little to the left of the lowest part to avoid the worst of the mud.

The path leads through a couple of stiles to the former railway embankment which now carries the Monsal Trail **(4)** (the tunnel between here and the Monsal Head viaduct is closed, and there is no access from the footpath which runs above this end of the tunnel). Walk left along the embankment for a few metres, take the steps down the other side and follow the path on down the valley. Cross a minor road, then later a major one, and turn left when you reach a third road. Keep right at the junction, and you will be back at the Ashford car park in about a quarter of a mile.

Alternative route

For an extra mile and a quarter, when you reach the railway embankment **(4)** turn left along it for about three quarters of a mile. You will reach a bridge over a major road with a road junction just to your right. Immediately beyond the bridge, take a path on the left which leads down to the road. Turn left under the bridge, go straight ahead at the road junction into the private road to Churchdale Hall, and follow the instructions for route 10 to Ashford. Walk through the village to return to the car park.

There is a very pleasant walk from Ashford through Great Shacklow Wood to the White Lodge car park, at the foot of Taddington Dale, and then on along Monsal Dale; but this is mentioned in several guidebooks so I shall not describe it here. The route is obvious from the OS map and is easy to follow.

Walk 10: Ashford and Bakewell

Start: Park near the old bridge just east of Ashford (SK199696), now superseded by a new one where the A6 bypasses the village. The bridge itself
is closed to traffic, but there is some parking space on the approach roads
at either end. Alternatively use the small car park at the other end of
Ashford village, though this soon fills up at weekends (there is sometimes
an overflow park adjacent). Or you can park in the road near the north
end of Lumford Bridge **(3)** (SK 116690), reached by a turning off the A619
Baslow road about a quarter of a mile from Bakewell bridge.

If you intend to follow the alternative route through the town of Bakewell,
you can park either in the town (the large park across the river usually
has space) or at the former Bakewell station where you join the Monsal
Trail (SK223690).

Distance: $4\frac{1}{4}$ miles (alternatives 5 and $5\frac{1}{4}$).

Public transport: The Manchester – Buxton – Bakewell – Derby – Nottingham service runs
every two hours, including Sundays. There are three or four buses a day
(including Sunday) on the Hanley – Buxton – Bakewell – Sheffield route,
three or four buses from Castleton (not on winter Sundays) which connect
with trains at Hope station, and three buses from Macclesfield on summer
Sundays. All these pass Ashford and Bakewell.

Amenities: There are several pubs and cafes in Ashford and more in Bakewell: also
the Cock and Pullet at Sheldon. There are toilets in the Ashford car park,
hidden in a back lane near the west end of the village, and in the centre
of Bakewell (where parking may be difficult).

This is a pleasant walk along the riverside meadows from the popular
village of Ashford-in-the-Water to the outskirts of Bakewell; then past
a packhorse bridge and back to Ashford over low hills, using a short
stretch of the Monsal Trail. There is about half a mile of road walking,
with a footway or grass verge. The route should be satisfactory in any
weather.

Although just off the main route, the picturesque Sheepwash Bridge
in the centre of Ashford is worth a look (you can see it from the A6
where it bypasses the village), and the Peak Park Information Centre in
the old Market House in Bakewell has a wide range of books, leaflets
and maps to interest walkers.

A Well-Dressing at Ashford

The Walk

If you started at the car park in Ashford, walk along the main street and cross the A6020 to reach the old bridge. Walk across it to the A6 road, turn left along it, and immediately go through a gate on the left **(1)**. Follow the obvious path which runs along the river valley. Where it reaches a residential street, go straight across. Soon after this the path reaches the A6 again. Turn left along it; the road is busy but there is a footway alongside.

In about a quarter of a mile **(2)**, turn left into the second factory entrance (Lumford Mill) and cross the river, then turn right along a road past houses until you see the end of the packhorse bridge (Lumford bridge) on your right; it is worth a short detour to look at it. (Alternatively, if you have not had enough of the A6, stay on it past the factory entrance and take the next turning on the left, a footpath which brings you over the packhorse bridge).

Take the turning opposite the end of the packhorse bridge **(3)**. This rough lane has the wall and outbuildings of Holme Hall on its right. Follow the road uphill, leaving various quarry buildings on your right. Beyond the last of these it swings right through a gate. Continue along the gravel track, through a field, until the track turns left; leave it and go straight ahead to a gate at the top of the field. Go through this and follow the walled lane, ignoring the footpath which diverges to the left. The track takes you over the top of the hill and down to the Monsal Trail **(4)**, the footpath which occupies the route of the old railway from London and Derby to Manchester which closed in 1965. The track is also open to cyclists and horses, so keep a good lookout.

Turn left along the trail for half a mile, over a road and under a stone bridge. Where the trail crosses over the next road **(5)**, take a path on the right just before the bridge which brings you down to the road. Go cautiously under the bridge, then straight on at the triangular junction into a private road (it is a right of way for walkers).

Follow the road for nearly half a mile to the gate of Churchdale Hall; bear left just before the gate, as signposted, and then right over a stile. Cross the field, with the gardens of the hall on your right, to another stile, and continue in the same direction over several more stiles until you reach a road (6). Turn left along it, and in a quarter of a mile you will reach the turning for Ashford village (7). If you parked in the village, turn right along the main street; otherwise take the turning on the left back to the old bridge.

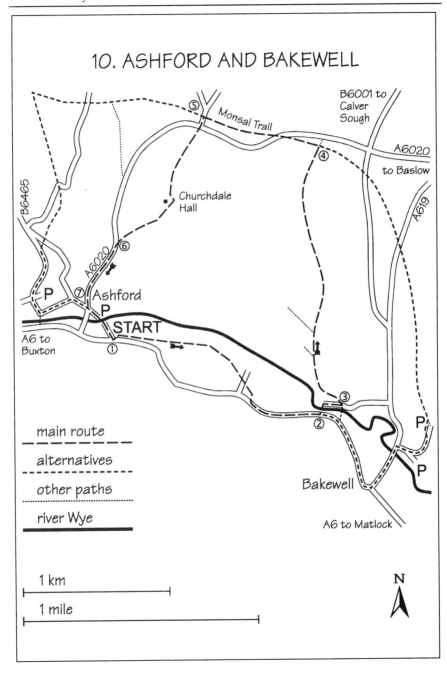

10. ASHFORD AND BAKEWELL

main route

alternatives

other paths

river Wye

1 km

1 mile

N

Alternative routes

If you want to visit Bakewell, go straight on along the A6 instead of crossing the river at Lumford Mill or Lumford Bridge; at the roundabout, turn left for the town centre and the information centre in the old Market House. Continue across the bridge, then turn right and fork left up the hill to reach the old station. Go just left of the station buildings to reach the Monsal trail, and turn left along it. In about a mile, after passing under two main roads, you will reach the main route **(4)**. Leave the trail, as described above, when you come to the second bridge over a main road **(5)**. This will add about a mile to your walk.

Another alternative is to continue for another half mile along the Monsal Trail after going over the second main road, under two bridges and onto an embankment, to where the footpath from Little Longstone crosses the trail on the level. Turn left along this, and follow the directions for the last part of Walk 9 to Ashford. If you parked at the bridge you will need to walk along the main street to return to it. This alternative is about three quarters of a mile longer than the main route.

Walk 11: Bakewell and Edensor

Start: At the car park at the former Bakewell railway station (SK222690), reached by crossing the river from the town centre and then turning right. At the top of the hill, bear left into the industrial estate (signed 'No through road') and then right into the car park. This car park is about half a mile from the town centre. It is not possible to park in Chatsworth Park, nor in Edensor village. One or two cars could park on the verge of the minor road east of Ballcross Farm where the Edensor lane joins it (SK235697).

If you intend to take the alternative route which passes near Calton Lees car park (SK259685) you can park there if it is more convenient for you. There is room to picnic there.

Distance: 4¼ miles (alternatives 4½ to 5½)

Public transport: There are good bus services to Bakewell (half a mile from the starting point) from Buxton and Matlock, with rail connections at both places, and also from Chesterfield, Derby, Manchester, Nottingham, Sheffield and Stoke-on-Trent and some other towns, as well as local services.

There is a very limited service, except Sunday, from Matlock to Baslow and Calver which passes Edensor village. Each Sunday there is a single bus, timed for walkers, from Ilkeston to Matlock and Buxton which passes Edensor, and on summer Sundays there are four buses from Chesterfield to Bakewell and one from Sheffield via Matlock to Crich which pass Edensor.

If you come to Bakewell by bus from Chesterfield or Sheffield, instead of walking back to Bakewell you can walk from near Edensor through Chatsworth Park (cross the bridge towards the house, then bear left) to Baslow and catch your bus there. The walk is pleasant and the distance is much the same.

Amenities: there are many pubs and cafes in Bakewell, though not at the station. There is no pub in Edensor but there is a cafe here and you can also get refreshments near Chatsworth House. There are toilets in Bakewell, at some of the car parks, but not at Bakewell Station; there are toilets at the garden centre adjoining the Calton Lees car park, but these may not be available outside business hours.

The walk starts at the former Bakewell Station and follows the Monsal Trail for a short way before climbing through Manners Wood to the grassy ridge of Calton Pastures. It then drops through New Piece Wood

Chatsworth Park

to Edensor (pronounced 'Ensor'), with a fine view of Chatsworth House across the river Derwent.

From Edensor a firm track, and then a very minor road, is followed back over the ridge to Ballcross farm, and then a path through the woods back to the starting point.

The public is free to walk at will in Chatsworth Park, by courtesey of the owners; so you can vary that section of the route to suit yourself, perhaps including a visit to the gardens or the home farm.

The walk is on gritstone and shale. Much of it is among trees, which will be at their best in spring or autumn. The way is suitable for all weathers, though the steeper paths are slippery when wet so care should be taken. About half a mile is along a quiet byroad.

The first half mile of this walk is shared with walk 12.

Please note that the map is drawn with East at the top, and the scale is distorted at the starting point to show the route more clearly. Details of Bakewell town have been omitted.

The Walk

From the station car park, go to the left of the handsome station building (now offices) and turn right, under the bridge, along the Monsal Trail.

This was until the 1960s the main railway line from London St. Pancras to Manchester Central. It closed when the West Coast route was electrified, and this section is now an all-weather path open to walkers and also to cyclists and horses.

Just before the next bridge **(1)**, go up the steps on the left and over the stile. Turn left and then bear right along a path which leads to an iron gate. Go over the stile beside it and continue along the path, which curves round to the left as it crosses a narrow part of a golf course. The path enters Manners Wood, where it is clear and stony but can be slippery when wet.

In a few hundred metres the path divides **(2)**. The clearer right-hand path passes a board telling you that it is a concessionary path (walk 12 goes this way); but you should take the left-hand path, which is rougher and climbs steeply through the wood, crossing another level track on the way. It crosses a small stream near a small stone shelter, and leaves the wood by a ladder stile over a stone wall.

You are now in the open grassland of Calton Pastures. Walk half right towards a clump of old trees, passing just to their right, and go straight on to a stile, ignoring the gateway on the right (this is not quite as on the OS map). Cross the wooden stile, which is waymarked, and go past the pond **(3)** and over another stile. Now bear well to the right, to a distant gate and stile just to the left of a small wood. On the way you will notice a broad curving grass track on your left which was once used as a racecourse.

Follow the broad level track, which eventually curves left towards a picturesque cottage; but before you reach it, just short of an iron barn, turn left at a footpath signpost and go over a step-stile beside a gate **(4)**. A short walled track leads down through New Piece Wood to a high step stile beside another gate. Cross it, and you will find a couple of seats where you can relax and enjoy the view **(5)**.

You are now in Chatsworth Park. The river Derwent is below you and beyond it is Chatsworth House, Derbyshire's most stately home. To its right are the fine gardens in which, in suitable weather, you can see the jet of one of the world's highest fountains. A little to the left, through the trees, is the spire of Edensor church.

The notice board by the gate tells you that you can roam at will in this part of Chatsworth Park, and you may take advantage of this (at the expense of an extra half mile or so) by heading down to the river to get a better view of Chatsworth House. Or you can cross the river by the bridge, just to the left of the house, to visit the gardens or the farm, which

11. BAKEWELL AND EDENSOR

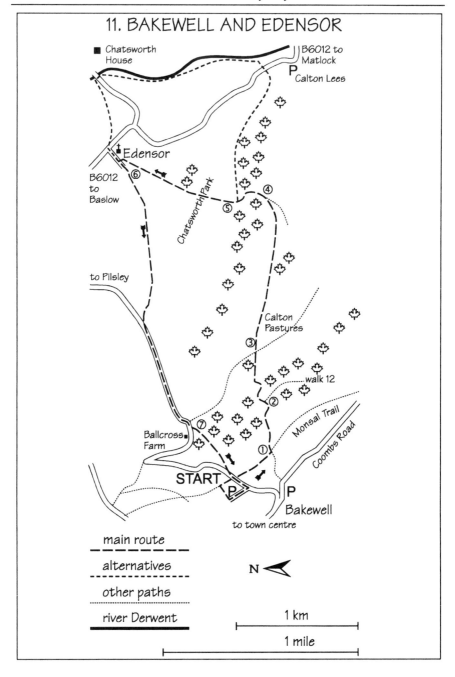

■ Chatsworth House

B6012 to Matlock

P Calton Lees

Edensor

B6012 to Baslow

⑥

Chatsworth Park

④

⑤

to Pilsley

Calton Pastures

③

walk 12

②

Monsal Trail

⑦

Ballcross Farm

①

Coombs Road

START

P

P

Bakewell

to town centre

main route

alternatives

other paths

river Derwent

N

1 km

1 mile

are open daily from Easter to October (there is a charge). The house is also open, but your boots are unlikely to be welcome. If you make this diversion towards the house, crossing the B6012, return to that road where it passes Edensor village and turn left up the village street by the church.

However, our main route leads from the seats at the park entry straight towards Edensor church spire, passing a few waymark posts with yellow arrows. Go to the left of a fenced wood; then as you approach the church, go rather to the left of the graveyard and you will find a complicated gate, stile and steps arrangement (6). This leads you by a stepped path down to the village street.

Turn left along the street (if you have been nearer to Chatsworth you will rejoin the route here). Edensor village used to be closer to Chatsworth House, but one of the Dukes of Devonshire did not want to see it from his windows, so he rebuilt it on the present site. The houses are obviously architect designed, but varied – perhaps the Duke ordered one of each design in the architect's pattern book.

The road becomes a firm walled track, and climbs steadily for a mile to join a very minor road. Continue straight ahead along this, over the top of the hill. A short way beyond the hilltop, near Ballcross farm, the road turns right (7). You can follow it down – it will be dry and easy going, but about half a mile further; but the more direct way is to go just round the bend (ignoring the path on the left which leads back over Calton Pastures) for a few metres, then look out for a footpath signpost almost hidden in the wood on your left, a few metres from the road. Follow the clear path which leads downhill from here, ignoring several cross paths. In about half a mile it will bring you to the road again; turn left, and immediately beyond the bridge turn right into the car park.

Alternative routes

I have already suggested that you can walk where you wish in Chatsworth Park, so you can choose whatever route you like from the point where you join the park to Edensor village. One possibility, at the cost of an extra mile or so, is to follow the edge of the wood to the right until the large car park at Calton Lees comes in sight. Then descend to the river bank and walk along it, passing Chatsworth House on the other bank, to the bridge and turn left to walk near the road to Edensor village.

Note that although you can see the lane by which you will leave Edensor from the point where you enter the park, you cannot cut across to it.

Walk 12: Manners Wood and the Monsal Trail

Start: At the car park at the former Bakewell station (SK222690), or alternatively (without much change to the distance) at the main Bakewell car park (SK220685) off Coombs Road, across the bridge from the town centre. Parking in the centre of Bakewell is possible, but difficult on market days and at the weekend.

Distance: 4¾ miles (alternatives 4 to 5).

Public transport: There are good bus services to Bakewell from Buxton and Matlock (with rail connections at both places) and from Chesterfield, Derby, Manchester, Nottingham, Sheffield , Stoke-on-Trent and other towns around the Peak District as well as many local services. You can shorten the walk by about a mile by catching a bus on the Matlock to Bakewell route (usually at least one bus each hour).

Amenities: Bakewell, the only town within the National Park and its administrative centre, has many pubs and cafes. There is an interesting Peak Park information centre in the old Market House on the road leading to the bridge : you can buy guide books and maps there. There are public toilets in Bakewell (near the information centre, and elsewhere), but not at the station car park.

The walk starts at the former Bakewell station, follows a concessionary path through Manners Wood, descends past Bowling Green Farm to the river Wye and returns along the Monsal Trail.

There is no road walking. Most of the way is along firm tracks. However there may be forestry work in progress in the wood, in which case part of the concessionary path may be churned up by vehicles; so boots are recommended in damp weather. There will be little view from the woodland path when the trees are in full leaf, so this walk is probably at its best in late autumn or early spring.

The Walk

From the station car park, pass to the left of the elegant station building (now in commercial use) and turn right under the bridge and along the Monsal Trail. This was once the Midland Railway main line from London St. Pancras to Manchester via Derby, which was closed (north of Matlock) in 1968 when the West Coast main line to Manchester was electrified. It is now an all weather footpath, open also to bicycles and horses, called the Monsal Trail after one of the dales that it runs through.

12. MANNERS WOOD AND THE MONSAL TRAIL

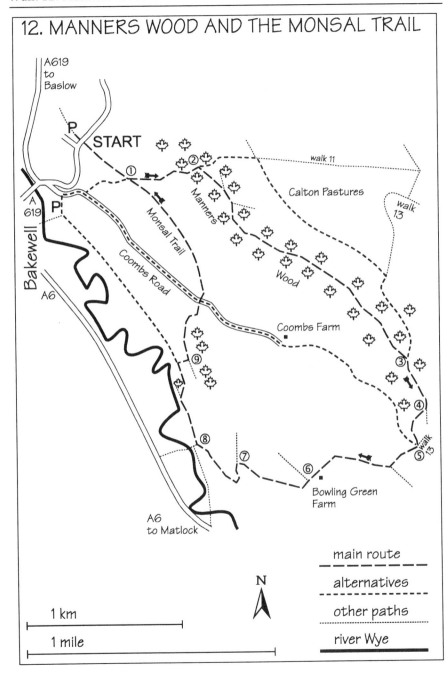

In a quarter of a mile you will reach a bridge over the trail (1). Go up the steps on the left just before the bridge, and over a stile; turn left and then bear right along an obvious green path leading up to an iron gate.

(If you start from the town, walk past the information centre and over the road bridge – which is well worth a closer look. Turn right and right again into Coombs Road, passing the main car park – or you may start the walk from there. In about 300 metres, there is a footpath sign by a gate on the left. Turn left up the tarmac drive, then right, and up the field side to a bridge over the Monsal Trail (1). At the end of the bridge, bear right along an obvious green path leading to an iron gate. You are now on the main route).

There are many stiles in the fence above you; ignore them, they are for the convenience of golfers retrieving misdirected balls. Go over the stile beside the iron gate, and continue along the green track which curves left round the hillside and climbs into Manners Wood. Within the wood the path is clear and stony. In a few hundred metres, just beyond a tiny stream, you will come to a path junction (2). The right-hand path, which you should take, has a notice board telling you that this is a concessionary path by courtesy of the Haddon estate. It is waymarked, although there are a couple of junctions where the marks are not obvious. This path is normally open, but may be closed occasionally for forestry or other work. If you should find it closed, fork left instead and follow the route described under 'alternatives' below.

Fairly soon you join another path; turn right along it, and keep right at the next fork. From here the way is obvious along a track which runs along the wooded hillside for over a mile, climbing gently at first and then levelling off. If the leaves are off the trees you will have glimpses of a view over the valley to your right.

The concessionary path ends (with another notice board) where a right of way joins from the left (3), but your way is along the track which continues straight ahead for a hundred metres further. At a fork (4), take the obvious right-hand track leading downhill – there is a faint blue arrow at the junction.

In a quarter of a mile you will reach a junction of tracks (5). Do not turn sharp right (unless you want the shorter alternative route) but turn half right along a well-used fenced track which climbs gently. Keep right at a junction (following the 'Bakewell' signpost), and follow the track as it descends past Bowling Green farm. A short way beyond the farm entrance the main track turns right (6), but your way is straight ahead down a green track (waymarked 'Bridleway'). On your left is a plain rectangular building, which probably had an ornamental parapet at one time, and the level lawn in front of it is presumably the former bowling green of Haddon Hall.

Where the track ends, in a hundred metres or so, go through a wicket gate on the right and follow the path alongside an iron fence through three more gates until you meet a tarmac farm road **(7)**. On the other side of the iron fence is the park of Haddon Hall; but the trees and the slope of the ground prevent you seeing the hall, although you can see a stone dovecot tower below you.

Turn left along the farm road and follow it downhill. It bends sharply around the mouth of a tunnel on the old railway line, but this part of the line is not open to walkers. So continue until you come close to the river Wye on your left **(8)**. At this point, bus travellers can make their way to the main road, either by continuing along the lane or by taking a path on the left, just before the river, which will bring you out near the entrance to Haddon Hall. But to return to Bakewell you should go through a wicket gate on the right, signposted 'Coombs Road'.

Follow the path through a long field, walking more or less parallel to the fence on your left. There are occasional waymrk posts. When you reach one which offers a choice of paths, take the right-hand one to pass just right of a small wood. (If you want the town car park or the centre of Bakewell rather than the station, you can take either path and just keep straight on until you reach the car park, where there is a footbridge leading to the town centre; but if the path is muddy, keep on the main route for the time being).

You will see a wire fence crossing the field ahead of you; make for a wicket gate at the right-hand end of it, beside a large wood **(9)**. Go through the gate and turn left along the firm track. In a quarter of a mile it reaches a tarmac road (Coombs Road) with an old railway bridge on the right. (For the town centre, go left along the road to reach the town in three quarters of a mile; or continue as described below to avoid road walking). Turn left for a few metres and then right, beside a gate which is inconspicuously waymarked. Go up the steep path to the Monsal Trail and turn left along it – you cannot turn right; this is the end of the trail. You will be back at the station car park in rather less than a mile. (For the town centre, at the first bridge over the railway go up the steps on the right, over the bridge, and down the obvious path to Coombs Road. Turn right for the car park and town centre).

Alternative routes

If the concessionary path is closed, or if the trees are in leaf and you would prefer a more open route, at the expense of an extra quarter of a mile, do not take the concessionary footpath but fork left where it starts. Continue up through the wood and on over the grass, passing just right of a clump of trees, to a gate near a pond. Here there is a junction of paths; turn half right and walk along a large field, parallel to the edge of the wood which is a couple of hundred metres down on your right. In half a mile a section of the wood projects towards the path; go along the left side of it till you reach a stile into the wood. Go over it and follow the obvious path, which shortly turns left, for nearly half a mile. Don't miss the point where the path bears right out of the clearing under the power lines. Eventually you will join a track **(3)**, at a point which tells you that the way on the right is the concessionary path through Manners Wood. Turn left instead, and you are back on the main route.

To shorten the walk to 4 miles; when you reach the junction of tracks at the end of Manners Wood **(5)**, turn sharp right instead of half right. You will reach the end of the Monsal Trail in a mile; just beyond the bridge, turn right beside a wooden gate. A short steep path brings you up to the trail; turn left along it, back on the main route.

You can buy a leaflet describing other walks around Bakewell at the Information Centre.

Monsal Trail near Bakewell

Walk 13: Calton Houses and Rowsley

Start: The large car park (free) at Calton Lees, on the B6012 at the south end of Chatsworth Park (SK259685).

A few cars could park in the village street at Rowsley (a cul-de-sac), but take care not to cause an obstruction. If you are visiting Caudwell's Mill, which is just beyond the main road at Rowsley (SK 256658), you could park there – the car park is just off the minor road to Stanton.

Distance: 4¾ miles (alternative 6½)

Public transport: There is a very limited service, except Sunday, from Matlock to Baslow and Calver which passes Calton Lees. Each Sunday there is a single bus, timed for walkers, from Ilkeston to Matlock and Buxton which passes Calton Lees, and on summer Sundays there are four buses from Chesterfield to Bakewell and one from Sheffield via Matlock to Crich which pass Calton Lees. All these buses turn off the A6 at Rowsley about 300 metres from the route of the walk at this point, so you can use the service to avoid the walk beside the river.

There is a good service along the A6 passing the end of Rowsley village street a few metres from the route of the walk: hourly buses from Derby, weekday and Sunday, with additional buses from Matlock on weekdays; and a bus every two hours or so on the 'Trans-Peak' Derby to Manchester route.

Amenities: There are two pubs in Rowsley and several pubs and cafes in Bakewell and Baslow. There is coffee shop in the garden centre by the Calton Lees car park, a cafe in Edensor, and refreshments outside Chatsworth House.

There are toilets at the garden centre, but these may not be available outside opening hours. There are toilets in Bakewell and near the crossroads in Darley Dale, along the A6 towards Matlock.

The walk starts at the south end of Chatsworth Park and climbs past estate houses onto the ridge which separates the Derwent and Wye valleys, and also the Chatsworth and Haddon estates. It descends the end of the ridge to Rowsley, near the confluence of the two rivers, and follows the Derwent back to the starting point.

Most of the route is through wood or green fields; about a quarter of a mile is along very quiet roads.

Old Railway Station at Rowsley

This is one for dry weather, as several stretches of the route can be muddy. I have walked it at the end of a very wet autumn and the mud didn't come over my boots, but it was a close thing! There are some fine views from this walk, so you will enjoy it most in reasonably clear weather.

The Walk

From the car park walk along the access road away from the main road, passing the garden centre entrance on the left and going through a 'No Through Road' gateway into a walled tarmac lane. Follow this round a bend to the right. Ignore a turning left and go straight ahead through a gate (blue waymark) and along a firm track up the valley.

In two-thirds of a mile this does a quick zig-zag and goes through a waymarked gate and between buildings (Calton Houses), and deteriorates into a walled footpath. This passes through a gate into a field **(1)**. Turn left, following the plantation wall on your left. At a waymark post you join a track; follow it left through a gate and up the hill. In a hundred metres or so a path forks left, marked by waymark posts. Follow this up hill, to a stile and gate into the wood near its right-hand end **(2)**.

13. CALTON HOUSES AND ROWSLEY

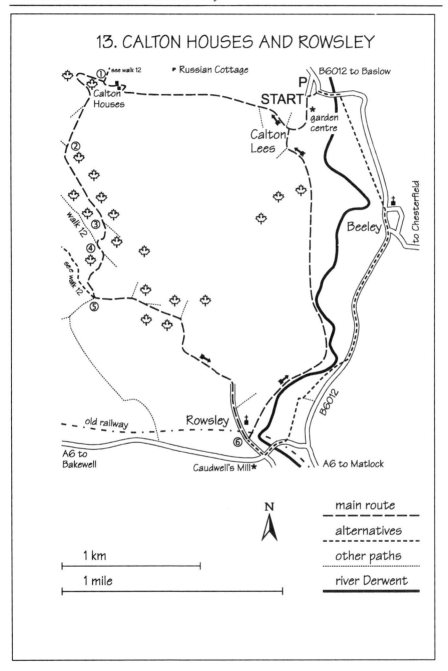

Look back at this point. On the ridge opposite you can see the picturesque 'Russian Cottage'; a little further left, on the hillside beyond, is the turreted tower above Chatsworth House. Further to the right is Beeley Moor, the eastern edge of the Pennines.

Now go over the stile and follow the clear path into the wood and leftwards along a clearing. Soon after you pass under the power lines, the path bears right out of the clearing at a waymark post. Before long it passes through a gateway in a substantial stone wall (the boundary between the Chatsworth and Haddon estates) and turns left alongside the wall **(3)**. Here you are at the top of the ridge, and there is a fine view (if the trees have not grown to block it) across the Wye Valley to Stanton Moor (with the radio mast), Harthill Moor, Youlgreave and, to the right in the valley, Bakewell – all places you can visit on other walks in this book.

The track, which may be muddy, leads downhill and to the right until it meets another track **(4)**. To the right is a concessionary path through Manners Wood, used in walk 12; but your way is left, along the track. In a hundred metres a waymarked track branches right, downhill. Take it, and in two or three hundred metres you will reach a junction of several tracks **(5)**.

Turn left, up a track between a hedge and a stone wall, and keep straight on where there are branch tracks on the left. In half a mile, at the end of the larch wood, you will reach a junction where the track is closed to vehicles by a metal barrier. Turn right down the firm walled track. In about a quarter of a mile this becomes the main street of the older part of Rowsley village. Pass the church and the abutments of an old railway bridge (Peak Rail have plans to restore it, so that they can re-open a further stretch of the old Midland line), and look out for a footpath signpost on the left **(6)**. (For buses go ahead to the main road, A6, for the main bus routes; turn left there, and left at the junction, for buses which pass Calton Lees car park).

Turn left along the indicated track (often muddy) under a railway bridge, and on alongside the river. The track becomes less clear where it enters a green field, but keep along the wall on your left and a stile will lead you into a path through a short scrubby wood. After another stile the path bears left, faintly visible, and comes close to the river at a bend. Beyond this it diverges from the river again, as a very straight path towards the lower end of a wood which spreads down the hillside. It goes through a muddy waymarked gateway and on to another which has both waymark and signpost, and was extremely muddy on my visit.

Now the path climbs the spur to go just right of the end of the wood, past a large tree, and then over a ladder stile on your left. Turn right alongside the wall. Ignore the first gate, but go over the stile beside the next gate onto the road. Turn right, through the picturesque estate village of Calton Lees, and right at the road junction, to return in a hundred metres or so to the car park.

Alternative routes

There is no opportunity to shorten this walk, but you can extend it to about 6½ miles. This extension is off the sketch map for this walk, but you can see it on the map associated with Walk 12.

At the gate into the field beyond Calton Houses (1), turn right and follow a track which at first runs alongside the wall and then bears uphill to a gate into a wood. Do not go through the gate, but turn left along a track. Beyond a gate and stile your path diverges slightly to the right of the track, towards a distant clump of trees, and as you approach it you will cross a stile and walk beside a pond to another stile. Go ahead, crossing another path, and just left of the trees, and follow the little valley down to a ladder stile which takes you into Manners Wood.

Follow the path down through the wood, until you reach a junction where the path on the left is signed as a concessionary path by courtesy of the Haddon Estate. This is the route of Walk 12; you could save about a quarter of a mile by following it till it rejoins the main route at another notice board (4) in rather more than a mile. But to keep that walk for another day, continue down the path to the bottom end of the wood, across a short strip of the golf course, through a gate and down to a bridge over the former railway which is now the Monsal Trail. Go over the stile just before the bridge to join the trail and turn left along it.

In half a mile you will reach a sign marking the end of the trail (beyond this the railway went through a tunnel, now closed). Go down the path on the right to the road (Coombs Road) and turn left under the bridge. Now follow the road for nearly a mile, passing Coombs Farm, to a junction where you rejoin the main route; this is point (5) on both sketch maps. Ignore the track sharp left (this is the main route) and turn left up a track with a hedge on the left and wall on the right – you are now back on the main route.

You can avoid the muddy stretch beside the Derwent, at the cost of a little extra distance and two-thirds of a mile of road walking, if at Rowsley you continue to the main road, turn left over the river and old railway and turn into the car park of the Grouse and Claret inn. Ahead of you is a low stone building; this was for a short time the terminal station of the railway from Derby, which was planned to pass through Chatsworth Park. When the Duke of Devonshire refused to allow this, the line was re-routed through Bakewell and this station became redundant. Fortunately it was preserved and is now a listed building, though the industrial buildings around it are derelict and may have gone by the time you read this.

Walk in front of the inn, through a gateway and across the inn's picnic field to a wooden stile and gate, and along a path parallel to a hedge. (The offical path is to the right of the hedge, although most walkers choose the other side at first; if you do go to the right, watch out for some unprotected holes). This area is being redeveloped, so the field may be built on but the path should remain.

In a couple of hundred metres the path runs between a fence on your left and the back of a new housing estate on your right. Where the fence ends, go over a stone stile on the right, and shortly bear left round the allotments on a clear path. This runs alongside the Derwent and then climbs the bank to join the road.

Walk carefully along the road to the left, passing the first turning to Beeley village in about half a mile. Opposite the next such turning, which runs past the church, go through a gate on your left and turn right along a clear straight track which brings you to Beeley Bridge. Turn left over it, and either follow the road back to the car park or take the obvious steep path which cuts the corner.

Walk 14: Beeley Moor

Start: At the Calton Lees car park and picnic area (SK259685), just off the B6012 near Beeley Bridge at the south end of Chatsworth Park. This car park is free and is very large, although popular, so you should be able to find space at any time. Alternatively, on a quiet day you could park carefully at the roadside in Beeley village.

If you approach from the east you can park at the roadside near the head of the Beeley Brook valley (SK286681) on the minor road from Chesterfield to Beeley, but this will mean that the later part of your walk is uphill.

Distance: 4 miles (alternatives 3½ to 5 miles).

Public transport: There is a very limited service, except Sunday, from Matlock to Baslow and Calver which passes Beeley and the Calton Lees car park. Each Sunday there is a single bus, timed for walkers, from Ilkeston to Matlock and Buxton which passes these points, and on summer Sundays there are four buses from Chesterfield to Bakewell and one from Sheffield via Matlock to Crich.

Amenities: Refreshments are available at the garden centre adjoining the Calton Lees car park, and in Edensor about a mile north and (when the house or gardens are open) at Chatsworth. There is an inn in Beeley village, a couple at Rowsley and several inns and cafes in Bakewell, Baslow sand Matlock.

There are public toilets at the garden centre adjoining the Calton Lees car park, although these may only be open during business hours.

The walk starts at the south end of Chatsworth Park; climbs to Beeley Moor by concessionary paths, with an optional extension to Hob Hurst's House at the top of the ridge; and returns down the narrow wooded clough of the Beeley Brook and through Beeley village. It is mainly on the gritstone of the Eastern Moors, though the lower part is on the shale of the Derwent valley.

Most of the way is suitable for all weathers. A part of the valley of the Beeley Brook may be slippery in wet weather, but this can be avoided. The walk is at its best in October and November when the autumn colours of the trees and bracken can be enjoyed.

The higher part of the walk is on concessionary paths, by courtesy of the Chatsworth Estate. These are usually open, but may be closed for a

Beeley Bridge

few days in the year. If so there will be signs at the points of access; but if you want to find out in advance you should ring the National Park information centre at Bakewell (01629-813227). The 3½ mile alternative route is entirely on rights of way and will not be affected by these closures.

Note that the sketch map is drawn with East at the top.

The Walk

Walk back to the road, either by the car park entrance or by the path at the far end of the car park near the garden centre gate. Turn right along the road, past the traffic lights and over the narrow bridge across the Derwent with its pedestrian refuges (you will get a better view of the bridge as you return). Walk up the road for a short way; where it bends to the right, go left into a minor road to the right of the lodge and park gate.

The road climbs steeply, with a good view over the wall on the left into a private section of the park; besides some fine old trees you will probably see pheasants and possibly deer. The tarmac ends at a large house (Beeley Hilltop) but the track continues. Just beyond the last farm

14. BEELEY MOOR

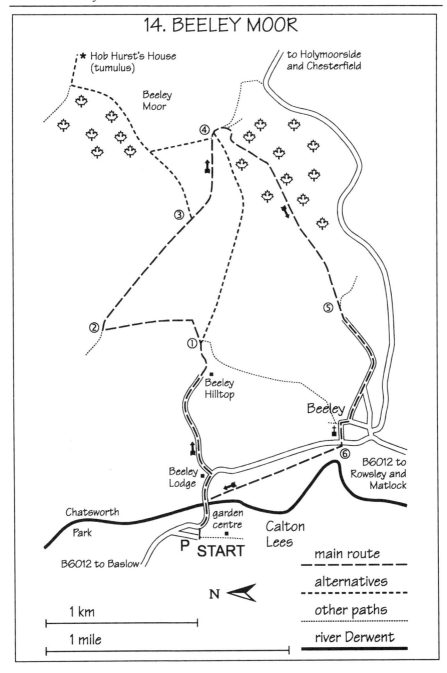

* Hob Hurst's House (tumulus)

to Holymoorside and Chesterfield

Beeley Moor

④

③

②

①

⑤

Beeley Hilltop

Beeley

⑥

B6012 to Rowsley and Matlock

Beeley Lodge

Chatsworth Park

garden centre

Calton Lees

P START

B6012 to Baslow

N

1 km

1 mile

– – – main route

· · · · · · alternatives

············ other paths

▬▬▬ river Derwent

building, cross a stone step stile on the left **(1)** and head half right across the field, in the direction indicated by the 'concessionary footpath' signpost. This brings you to a very high stone step stile, but you may find that the gate alongside is unlocked.

Turn left along a well-trodden path through the bracken, climbing gently. You can see the spire of Edensor (pronounced 'Ensor') church to the left, but Chatsworth house is hidden by the trees. In autumn the tree colours seen from this point are particularly fine.

When the path reaches a gravel track **(2)**, turn right along it; it is signed 'Footpath to open country' and is another concessionary route. The track runs very straight and climbs gently over rough grassland. After about half a mile a waymarked path forks left **(3)**; do not take it unless you want to follow the extension of the route to Hob Hurst's House, but continue along the track over the summit and down to a gate where you join a walled track **(4)**.

Turn left along this, across a branch of the Beeley Brook, then almost at once squeeze past a gate on the right. The path runs level at first, with a fine view over the wooded valley. Where it starts to climb, fork right down a narrower but clear path alongside the fence. Soon it becomes rougher and steeper. The OS map shows a wide zig-zag here, but it is not apparent on the ground. The path continues more steeply down through the trees, and this section may be slippery in wet weather. Ignore a cross path, but a short way beyond it turn right among scattered rocks; do not go down to the stream, but keep above the steepest part of the slope on a path, not very clear when the leaves have fallen, which runs almost level along the valley side. This gradually becomes clearer, and turns into a firm track which descends gradually, keeping well up the side of the valley.

Where the track forks, keep straight on rather than branching right. At a gate the track leaves the wood, but continues downhill with the wood just over the wall on your left. Where it nears the valley bottom it joins a farm drive **(5)**, and this soon becomes a tarmac road leading in half a mile to Beeley village.

Walk straight through this attractive village. At a little green, with a welcome seat under a tree (and the village pub down the road to the left), turn right and then left again past the church. At the main road **(6)**, go straight across and through the gate opposite, then turn right along a clear firm track through an outlying part of Chatsworth park. The curious green domes belong to the water pipeline from the Derwent dams to Derby and beyond.

The path brings you to Beeley Bridge, and you get a better view from this level. It was built in 1761 to replace an older bridge a short way upstream, although the high arch and the ribs beneath it make it look older. Turn left over the bridge to return to the Calton Lees car park.

Alternative routes

You can add a pleasant extra mile by visiting Hob Hurst's House at the top of the ridge, although you will have to retrace your steps for much of the way. The 'house' is in fact the remains of a prehistoric burial mound, of considerable interest to archaeologists; for the rest, the diversion is worth while for the visit to the heather covered moor and the view north and east from the top.

Follow the main route as far as the straight track which climbs across the rough grassland, but about half a mile after joining it take a waymarked concessionary path on the left **(3)**, signed 'Footpath to open country'. This aims for the left end of a long wood. On reaching it, the path turns right over a step stile (the gate beside it is usually padlocked) and then bears left alongside the wall enclosing the wood. It climbs steadily up onto the moor; to the right is a small rocky escarpment, the first of the 'edges' overlooking the Derwent valley which become far more impressive further north. At the top, a sign tells you that you are now in open country, and you soon reach a track. This is an old packhorse route, now a concessionary path; right brings you eventually to Holymoorside and Chesterfield, left to the Baslow to Chesterfield road near the Robin Hood Inn. We are not going so far, but if you walk a hundred metres to the right you will reach Hob Hurst's House, surrounded by concrete pillars and with an interpretation board to tell you all about it.

While you are here, admire the view north and east. To the north you can see the first of the impressive 'edges' overlooking the valley, and with sharp eyes you may be able to pick out the Nelson and Wellington monuments on them – respectively an obelisk and a cross. To the east the moor continues, with Chesterfield hidden beyond it.

Now return by the way you came. Shortly beyond the step stile, cross a bridge of wooden sleepers and then take the left-hand of the two waymarked paths, marked 'Beeley'. In a few hundred metres this will bring you to the gravel track which is the main route; turn left along it and you will very soon reach the walled track **(4)** and the valley of the Beeley Brook.

You can shorten the walk by half a mile by omitting the concessionary paths over the moor; you may have to do this on the rare occasions when these paths are closed. When you pass Beeley Hilltop farm, ignore the footpaths and continue up the walled track to the head of the brook **(4)**, nearly a mile on; then squeeze past the gate on the right and continue on the main route.

After rain, the steepest section of the path down the Beeley Brook valley may be slippery where it descends through the trees. Well-soled boots should cope; but to avoid this section, turn right when you reach the walled track and follow it down to Beeley Hilltop and return to the car park by the way you came.

Pheasants

Walk 15: King Sterndale and Cowdale

Start: Park on the wide grass verge of the Harpur Hill to King Sterndale road, near the junction with the Cowdale road (SK082713); this is about two miles south-east of the centre of Buxton.
Alternatively, park carefully near the bus turning circle at Burlow (SK071705), but take care not to obstruct the road. There is room for only one or two cars up the quarry road, between the old railway embankment and the gate. Or park on the grass verge near the road junction at Brierlow Bar, though this may be muddy after rain.
It is not possible to park on the A6 in Ashwood Dale, near the junction with Kid Tor Dale and Cowdale (SK086721). One or two cars can park beside the Cowdale road close to this junction, but the road is narrow and you should take care not to cause an obstruction.

Distance: 4½ miles (alternatives 2¼ to 4¾ miles). (Non-circular alternative routes, starting at Burlow or Brierlow Bar bus stops and ending in Buxton: 3½ to 5½ miles).

Public transport: There are infrequent weekday buses along the A515 (passing the turning for King Sterndale and also Brierlow Bar crossroads), on the Buxton to Hartington route. On Sundays there are buses from Sheffield, Mansfield, Derby and (in summer only) Chapel-en-le-Frith and Macclesfield passing these points, timed to allow a day out. There is a two-hourly service on the A6, stopping at the bottom of Cowdale, on the Nottingham – Derby – Buxton – Manchester route, and also several buses on the Sheffield to Buxton route and (except winter Sundays) the Chesterfield to Buxton route. There are additional buses on summer Sundays. Note that the Hanley to Sheffield bus runs non-stop along this part of its route, so Hanley walkers must change in Buxton.
A half-hourly bus service (hourly on Sundays) runs from the centre of Buxton and the railway station to the terminus at Burlow, just south of Harpur Hill, which is on the route of the walk. It passes Buxton Hospital, near the end of the Duke's Drive, which is on the alternative route back to Buxton.
If you take the bus from Buxton to either Burlow or Brierlow Bar, when you reach Cowdale you can walk into Buxton via Staden and the hospital instead of returning to your starting point.

Amenities: There are many pubs and cafes, and also toilets, in Buxton. You can also eat at the Church Inn, opposite the church at the far end of Chelmorton village.

This walk passes briefly through the industrial surroundings of Burlow two miles south of Buxton (Burlow is not named on the OS map, but is just south of Harpur Hill where there is a road junction, each road going under a railway bridge, and a cluster of houses). It follows a short stretch of old railway line and crosses the fields to Brierlow Bar, which takes its name from a former tollgate on the Buxton to Ashbourne road. From here it explores several short dry dales near to Buxton: Brierlow Dale, Kidtor Dale and Cow Dale. It is entirely on limestone, and should be passable in any weather. There may be mud on the stretch alongside the railway line beyond Burlow, but you can avoid this by using the road from Burlow to Brierlow bar.

About a mile is along a very quiet byroad and a further half mile along a road which is a little busier, with a grass verge. Two-thirds of the walk is within the National Park or along its boundary, the rest just outside it in the quarry area south-east of Buxton.

The walk is perhaps best when the leaves are off the trees, or just falling, as Kidtor Dale is heavily wooded and trees obscure the best of the view in Cow Dale.

At the head of Cow Dale is the tiny village of Cowdale; do not confuse it with Cowlow on the other side of the A6.

The walk is on the 'West' side of the White Peak map.

Kidtor Dale

The Walk

Walk south-west along the road from your starting point, across the main road and under the railway, to Burlow where there is a bus turning circle at the road junction. Turn left, and then right along a curving road with signboards for a quarry and various other businesses. The road goes through a gap in an old railway embankment and comes to a gate (1). Go over the ladder stile on the left, alongside the gate, and half-left across the field to another stile which brings you onto the route of the old railway. This was part of the Cromford and High Peak line, which was built in 1831 to join the Cromford Canal not far from Cromford to the Peak Forest canal at Whaley bridge. This part of the line ceased to be a through route in 1892 when the Ashbourne to Buxton line replaced it, but it remained in use for quarry and colliery traffic for some years longer.

Turn right, through a curving cutting. After a quarter of a mile the cutting is blocked by a fence, because it converges with a railway still in use for quarry traffic. The footpath climbs the bank on the right, with a handrail, though if it is muddy you may prefer to scramble more steeply up the bank. Now go through the gap in the wall and turn left. Continue alongside the railway, keeping a little way to the right at first to avoid a muddy patch.

Ignore a bridge over the railway, but go on into a dip (with a quarry tip on the right) and up again, through a kissing gate, then left under the railway (2). Go through another kissing gate and then steeply down the bank on your left. The path is faint, but your way is just to the left of the rocky end of a low ridge. Continue in the same direction, aiming about fifty metres to the right of a gateway and past an electricity pole, to a very inconspicuous step stile which leads you into the corner of the next field.

Go diagonally across the field, aiming for the Brierlow Bar garage which you can see ahead of you near the road junction, and through a gate, and on to another gate just left of the road junction. There is a step stile by a footpath sign just right of the gate, but it is damaged so you may need to use the gate.

Now turn right for a few metres to the road junction, then left, and left again along the A515 main road towards Buxton. In about fifty metres, cross the road to the entrance of Brierlow Bar Farm and go through the squeezer stile (with metal bar) just to the left of the gate (3).

15. KING STERNDALE AND COWDALE

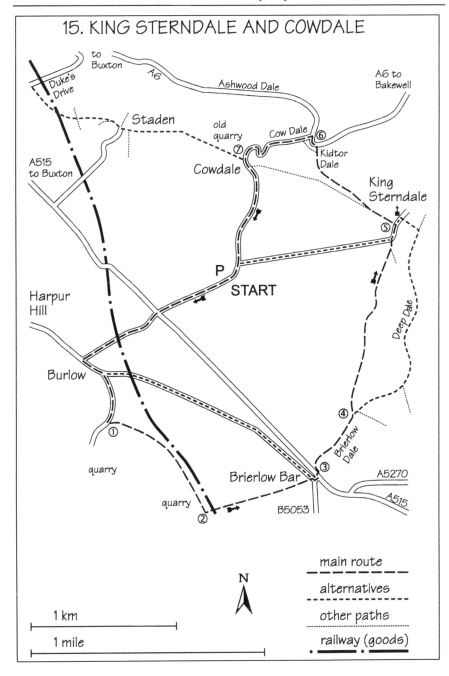

The path runs left for a few metres and then curves right to go down the short dry Brierlow Dale.

In about a quarter of a mile a similar dale joins on the left, and there is a cross wall in front of you (4). A few metres before this cross wall, go over an inconspicuous step stile in the wall on your left. Now follow the faint path which heads half right steeply up the dale side, passing just to the right of a small rock outcrop and curving round to a squeezer stile (again with an iron bar) on the skyline.

Cross the stile and bear half right, diagonally across the field, to a waymarked wooden stile in the far corner. Continue in the same direction, near to the wall on your left, through a gateway at the far left corner of the field, and straight on again towards the highest clump of trees. (It is possible that these will have been felled and replanted). A short way to the right of the trees you will find a waymarked gateway. Beyond this a clear track leads through another waymarked gate and stile, and on alongside a wall and tree belt on your left. Eventually it turns left through the trees to the road at the beginning of King Sterndale village. Turn right along the road, noting the broad verges – this is typical of the roads laid out at the time of the enclosure of open land in the 19th century.

In about a hundred metres, where the road starts to bear right, go through a wicket gate on the left (waymarked 'Midshires Way') into open parkland (5). Follow the faint path which runs alongside the fence on your left towards a distant stile; but before reaching the stile, fork right to cross a small ladder stile about fifty metres to the right, alongside a gate and sheep pen.

The stile leads onto a track, perhaps an old drive to King Sterndale Hall, which descends through a limestone cutting and then joins Kid Tor Dale, a short wooded dry dale which is rarely visited. At first there are rocky cliffs (the one on the right is Kid Tor), but the slopes ease as you reach the foot of the dale where it joins Ashwood Dale and the main road (6). Turn left and walk cautiously along this busy road for a hundred metres, and turn left into the minor road up Cow Dale. (An unofficial path through the trees, just short of the main road, avoids the main road walking; but it is rough and in places muddy). The river Wye runs at the other side of the main road, but take great care if you cross to look at it.

Follow the quiet road up Cow Dale, which is rather like the dale you came down – wooded, with limestone cliffs as you get further up the dale. Eventually the road steepens and zigzags to reach the dale head, with a fine view back down the dale when the leaves are off the trees. It levels out, and passes a house and a quarry track on the right. Beyond this point you can go through a stile by a footpath signpost on the right (**7**) to reach Staden and Buxton, but the main walk follows the road through the tiny village of Cowdale and up the hill for half a mile to the road junction. Keep right to return to your car.

Alternative routes

You can walk straight from the bus turning circle at Burlow to Brierlow Bar along the road. It is not too busy and has an adequate grass verge all the way. This will save you about half a mile, and avoid a part of the walk which will have muddy patches after rain.

For a short walk (2¼ miles), walk eastwards from your starting point along the very straight road towards King Sterndale. At the first bend the main route joins from your right; continue along the road for a hundred metres and then go through the wicket gate (waymarked 'Midshires Way) on your left (**5**).

If you have not visited Deep Dale (walk 16), it is well worth extending this walk by perhaps a quarter of a mile to take in the best stretch of it. In this case, after going down Brierlow Dale go over the stile in the wall ahead of you instead of the one on your left (**4**). Continue down the bottom of Back Dale, which is pleasant though not spectacular, for half a mile until it meets Deep Dale at a footpath signpost.

Turn left down Deep Dale; it become deep and narrow and the path rough underfoot, as it is largely over broken rock. The best path runs rather to the right of the bottom of the dale, and passes an impressive cave quite high in the dale side. It then descends to the dale bottom and there is a crossing of paths (the Midshires Way crosses the dale). Go over the footbridge and stile on the left. In wet weather there is a stream here which can be a little difficult to cross; it is best to make for the point where it runs through the old stone wall, a few metres downstream.

Now follow the path, half right, which zigzags up the dale side to a wooden stile and wicket gate at the top. Go straight ahead, with the wall on your right, up two fields linked by a rather unusual step stile, at the corner of the sheep pens. Three stiles close together bring you out on the road opposite King Sterndale church, which though not old would be attractive if it were not for a badly placed chimney. Turn left along the road for about a hundred metres. Where it starts to bend left, go through a wicket gate on the right **(5)** (marked 'Midshires Way'). You are now back on the main route.

If you came to this walk by bus, you can walk back to Buxton (or to the regular bus route at Buxton hospital) by way of Staden instead of completing the circular route. As you come into Cowdale village, and before reaching the green, look out for a footpath sign on the right **(7)**. Go through the squeezer stile by it, in the angle of the wall at the drive of the first house.

A clear path leads through a tree belt and crosses a step stile into a long narrow field. Walk the length of this field and the next, keeping alongside the fence on your right; a short way beyond this is a large quarry, disused except that spoil heaps at the far side are being re-worked. At a gateway and stile the fence bears slightly left and you keep alongside it, making for a group of buildings. Go over a waymarked stile and straight ahead up a green track, to pass to the left of a large barn and reach the end of the tarmac road at the hamlet of Staden.

Do not turn left along the tarmac, but go straight ahead with a white-painted garden fence on your right and through a stile by an iron gate (there are occasional 'Midshires Way' waymarks). Follow the track, with a wall on your right, but where the track bears left go straight ahead through an iron gate leading into a walled path. Cross a drive to a gate opposite, onto a green path which leads towards the railway viaduct. It passes under the left arch of the viaduct, where there is a wooden gate. Through this, go straight ahead to join a track descending from a group of houses on your left. Follow the track to the road (Duke's Drive). The main Buxton to Ashbourne road and the bus route are a few metres to your left; most buses come down the side road opposite. You will have walked about 3½ miles from Brierlow Bar or 4½ from Burlow. It is a mile further to the town centre; or you can use the regular bus service to the town centre and railway station.

Walk 16: Horseshoe Dale and Deep Dale

Start: Park at SK099699 on the Brierlow Bar to Chelmorton road, A5270, about
                       half a mile east of Brierlow Bar (which is the crossroads three miles from
                       Buxton on the Ashbourne road A515), near where the road dips and
                       bends across the head of Horseshoe Dale. There are several safe
                       parking spots on the broad grass verge.

Distance: 3½ miles (alternatives 2½ to 4¾)

Public transport: 3 to 6 buses a day (but none on Sunday) run from Buxton to Chelmorton
                       past the starting point. More buses pass Brierlow Bar, half a mile from
                       the start; about 5 a day on the Buxton to Hartington route and one or two,
                       on Sundays only, on the Sheffield or Chesterfield to Buxton route. Most
                       of these connect with the railway to Manchester, and with other buses,
                       at Buxton. On summer Sundays there are also buses, timed for a day
                       out, from Huddersfield and from Mansfield and Derby.

                       There is a better service on the A6 past the Topley Pike quarry, a quarter
                       of a mile off the route: for details see walk 8. Using this service together
                       with that to Brierlow Bar or Chelmorton makes a one-way walk of about
                       2 miles possible.

Amenities: There are good pubs in Chelmorton, Flagg and Taddington, as well as
                       the Duke of York on the A515 a couple of miles SE of Brierlow Bar, and
                       there are many pubs and cafes in Buxton.

                       The nearest toilets are at Miller's Dale station, beyond the A6, or on the
                       approaches to Buxton.

There are at least two Deep Dales in the Peak District; this is the one
north-west of Chelmorton. It is an impressive dale, mostly dry and with
interesting caves, but spoilt at its foot (where it runs into the Wye) by
the active workings of Topley Pike quarry. In spite of this it is worth
more attention than it gets. The return is over the fields near the edge
of the dale. There are only a couple of hundred metres of road walking,
with a grass verge.

If snow has fallen and drifted, the walled tracks used on the return
part of the main route tend to be choked by drifts. If so, the longer of
the two alternative routes may be easier walking.

This walk is on the 'West' side of the White Peak map.

Deep Dale

The Walk

Walk to the bottom of the dip in the road where there is a footpath signpost, and take the wicket gate just right of a barn; pass through the yard and another gate, and continue down the dale. This is Horseshoe Dale. Where the track swings right into a side dale (Bullhay Dale – you will notice the entry to a mine level, but this is on private land) keep on down the main dale.

In half a mile, Back Dale comes in on the left **(1)**, with a signpost; carry on down the main valley, which is now Deep Dale. The dale narrows and deepens as it comes to a bend. The path in the dale bottom is very rough (and becomes a stream in wet weather) but there is a better path just above the scree on the right. This leads past the wide mouth of a cave, high on the valley side, which makes a convenient and sheltered spot for a rest. Another cave can be seen high on the opposite side of the dale. Neither can be followed far.

A short way beyond the cave another footpath, from King Sterndale to Chelmorton, is crossed **(2)**; but unless you want to shorten the walk, keep on down the dale. Again the best path is to the right of the dale bottom. Eventually the path climbs alongside an earth bank and slurry

16. HORSESHOE DALE AND DEEP DALE

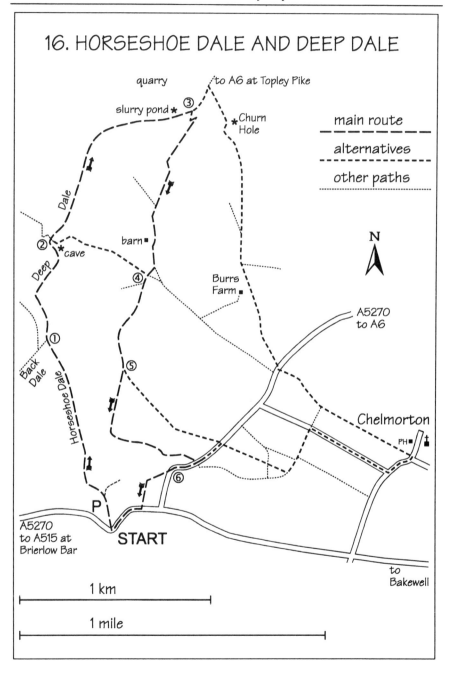

pond, and the quarry is seen on the left. This is one of the largest quarries still working within the National Park, and is well screened from most directions.

Where the path starts to descend at the end of the slurry pond and approaches overhead cables, **(3)**, join a faint path climbing diagonally back up the dale side. When it reaches the top, it doubles back to the left for a few metres to a step stile, which you cross. (If drifted snow is lying, you may find the longer alternative route described below is easier going).

Make for the furthest, highest corner of the field, where there is an isolated tree and a junction of overhead cables, and cross the step stile which is a few metres to the right of the corner. Turn left along a walled green lane. In a quarter of a mile, a short way beyond a ruined barn, is a junction of lanes; turn right (as indicated by a 'Midshires Way' waymark post), but continue ahead along the lane when the Midshires Way goes over a stile **(4)** (it crosses the dale just below the cave). At a fork in another quarter mile **(5)** you can go either way but the right-hand lane, through an iron gate, is slightly easier. Either way, turn right when you reach the road in another quarter mile.

The road dips to cross the head of Bullhay Dale; where it rises again and bends left **(6)**, cross a stile on the right (you can continue along the road if you prefer, turning right at the junction; it is very little further). Do not take the track which descends into the dale, but bear left across the field (no visible path) towards a farm. When you come in sight of a wall, look for the step stile, some metres left of a farm gate, and cross it. Then follow the wall on your left (my copy of the OS map shows the path on the wrong side of this wall) to another step stile, and turn right along the road for a couple of hundred metres to your starting point.

Alternative routes

For a shorter walk, immediately after passing the cave turn right up a clear footpath **(2)** (forming part of the Midshires Way) which zigzags very steeply up the dale side to a wooden stile. Follow a faint green path, and in 50 metres go over a step stile on your right. Aim to the right of an isolated tree, just left of an electricity pole, to the next step stile and continue in the same direction over two more. This brings you to a walled lane at a 'Midshires Way' waymark post **(4)**. Turn right along the lane, and you are back on the main route.

For a longer alternative, continue down the slope past the slurry pond

(3) to a wall gap at the dale bottom, and turn right up a short side dale. Towards the end of it, approaching a cave ('Churn Hole'), the path crosses an old wall and climbs very steeply up the head of the dale to a wooden stile. Follow the wall on your left till it turns away at a footpath signpost, and go straight ahead to join a farm track. Where this turns sharp left go straight ahead over a wooden stile, through the left-hand wall gap and over another stile, passing left of a farmhouse, to join a walled track at a stile beside an iron gate. Where the walls end go straight on, over a step stile just right of a gate, after which the track becomes walled again and you soon reach the road.

You can turn right alongside the road (there is a broad grass verge) to rejoin the main route before it crosses Bullhay Dale **(6)**. This will make the walk about 3¾ miles. But to visit Chelmorton at the cost of another mile, cross the road and take the lane opposite into the pleasant village whose main street is a cul-de-sac ending at the church and inn. Turn right along the street for a short way and then right along a by-road; in a quarter mile turn left along a walled track, which turns sharp right to reach the A5270 road a short way above the track used by the main route. Turn left along the road, across Bullhay Dale **(6)**, and follow the main route directions.

If you came from Buxton by bus, you can continue down Deep Dale beyond the slurry pond **(3)**, turn left at the dale bottom, and walk past the quarry to the main Derby to Buxton road, A6, at Topley Pike, where you can catch a bus back to Buxton.

Walk 17: Chelmorton, Five Wells and Blackwell

Start: In Chelmorton village; park at the side of the quiet main street of the village (a cul-de-sac) near the church (SK115702). Alternatively you could park on the verge of A5270 near its junction with A6 (SK116720), or on the verge of the very quiet road in Blackwell village.

If you propose to take the alternative route you can park in the Wye Dale car park opposite Topley Pike quarry entrance (SK104725), though this may be full at weekends.

Distance: 4 miles (alternatives 3½ to 4½, or 6 if combined with Walk 5).

Public transport: There are three to six buses a day (except Sunday) to Chelmorton from Buxton; some run through from New Mills. These buses pass Buxton station.

On the A6, stopping near both points where the route of the walk crosses, there are seven buses a day (including Sundays) on the Nottingham-Derby-Buxton-Manchester route and six (three on Sunday) on the Sheffield-Buxton route. On weekdays there are two on the Chesterfield-Tideswell-Buxton route.

Amenities: The Church Inn in Chelmorton is at the starting point of the walk, and the Waterloo Inn is on the A6 not far from the point where the route crosses it. There is also the Queens Head in Taddington, and various inns and cafes in Tideswell and Buxton.

There are toilets at the Millers Dale car park (SK138732) and in Tideswell and Buxton. Although there are no public toilets in Chelmorton, those at the Church Inn are accessible from outside and could no doubt be used in an emergency.

This walk starts from the quiet village of Chelmorton; visits (optionally) a prehistoric tomb; then leads by way of Blackwell to the rim of Chee Dale. After ascending an attractive side valley there is a choice of returning by the roadside or by a quiet path through farmland. A stretch of two hundred metres on the verge alongside a main road is unavoidable.

About a mile of the route is shared with Walk 5; you could combine the two into a walk of about 6 miles.

The walk is on the 'West' side of the White Peak OS map.

Chelmorton church

The Walk

Walk up to the end of Chelmorton village street, past the churchyard, and turn right up a steep stony track. A short way up on the left you will see the old village well, a spring flowing into stone troughs. Where the track levels out it passes through a long field heavily disturbed by lead mining. Halfway along this field the path forks; you can take either, but the left path saves a few metres.

The path reaches a lane by a wicket gate **(1)**. Ignore the farm drive ahead and turn left along a firm walled track (Pilwell Lane). In about a quarter of a mile, beyond the crest of the hill, it reaches an iron gate **(2)**. Your route is through the gate, but if you are interested in archaeology you may make a diversion (about a quarter of a mile) along a concessionary path to the Five Wells chambered cairn. This is a neolithic burial mound in which the stone chambers, now exposed, are well preserved. Like most such tombs it stands in a prominent position, facing east. To reach it, go through the signposted squeezer stile on the right just before the iron gate; go along the field, through a wall gap at the end, and on alongside the wall on the right till you see the stones of the tomb showing over the wall. Just before you reach it, there is a

17. CHELMORTON, FIVE WELLS AND BLACKWELL

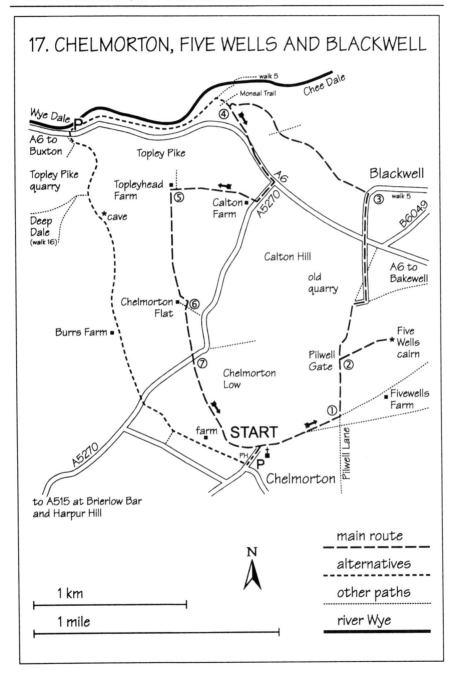

main route

alternatives

other paths

river Wye

N

1 km

1 mile

stile in the wall which gives access to the tomb. Return the same way to the lane and go through the iron gate **(2)**.

Follow the track that winds down to another gate. To your left, an old quarry has been infilled and may be all grassed over by the time you read this, though still untidy at my last visit. There is no way through it, even though the OS map shows Senners Lane at both sides of it. So turn right along the tarmac road, turning left with it at a junction (if you want to visit the Waterloo inn, go straight ahead there and then right at the main road). At the main road, cross carefully and go down the minor road straight opposite to the hamlet of Blackwell. Where the road turns right, go left over a stile by a gate into a walled track. (If you are combining this walk with walk 5, turn right along the road; at the next bend turn left into the Blackwell Hall drive and you are on the route of that walk).

Follow the track to its end, go over the stile and almost straight ahead alongside a ruined wall. Where this ends, continue ahead towards the vast quarry that you can see in Great Rocks Dale, with a railway line (once the main London-Derby-Manchester route) below it. Cross a stile near the field corner. Turn left along a gravel track for a few metres, then turn right just before the wall and follow the wall to a step stile near its far end. Go ahead, near the wall on your right, to a wooden stile which leads onto the rim of Chee Dale.

Here you are in a nature reserve; there are drifts of cowslips in late spring, and a scattering of purple orchids as well. Your route is to the left alongside a wall, but first (if you have a reasonable head for heights) go ahead for a few metres for a spectacular view both ways along the rocky Chee Dale; here you are on top of a cliff which drops sheer into the dale. The row of buildings to your left is Blackwell Cottages, once the home of railwaymen when the Buxton branch joined the main line just below you.

The path soon reaches the edge of a side valley and descends a rocky path to the right. Watch out for the point where it doubles back to the left and drops steeply to a stile in the valley bottom **(4)**, as the way straight ahead leads only to a precipice. Cross the stile (the route of walk 5 rejoins here) and walk left up the side valley, again full of cowslips in May, until you reach the main A6 road. You must follow this to the left for about 200 metres; the road is busy, but there is a grass verge although this is not very wide. At the road junction turn right into the Harpur Hill road, A5270.

You can follow this road for two thirds of a mile to its highest point

(7), where you go through a gate (with blue waymark) on your left; traffic is only moderate and there is a good grass verge. However the main route, about half a mile longer, is through farmland; it is little used although several of the stiles are new. For this route, soon after the road junction turn into a farm entrance on your right (no signpost). Follow the firm track to the right of all the farm buildings, but where it swings left go straight ahead through an iron gate. Go down the field towards the next farm, with a wall on your right. At the corner of the field cross this wall by a stile, go half left for a few metres to another stile, and walk past the left end of the farmhouse. Opposite the house, just before a cylindrical gas tank, go over a step stile on your left **(5)**. Then go across the field, bearing slightly right past a pond, to a step stile beside an iron gate. Follow the wall on your left almost to the cross wall. Then go over a wooden stile on your left and turn right.

At the next wooden stile, bear slightly left towards the farmhouse whose roof you can just see. When the next wall comes in sight, make for the field corner in front of a large building and cross the stile on the left there. Walk alongside the fence on your right; ignore the first gate but go through the second (waymarked), by a concrete trough, and on with a fence on the right to a stile which leads onto the farm drive **(6)**.

Cross the drive to a waymark post and go half left to a stile. Now follow the wall on your right, and keep with it as it shortly turns left. Where it ends, go straight ahead to a squeezer. Through this go straight on up the field to a wooden stile which gives onto the road **(7)**. (The more direct route along the road joins here).

Go straight across the road and through a gate with a blue waymark. Go on with the wall on your right, passing through another gate, and in about half a mile you will be back at your starting point at the top of Chelmorton village street.

Alternative route

You can extend the walk by about half a mile by walking up the foot of Deep Dale, past the entrance to Topley Pike quarry; part of this route is shared with the longer alternative route of Walk 16.

When you descend from the rim of Chee Dale and cross the stile in the side valley **(4)**, turn right instead of left and follow the path down, across the old railway, until it passes a brick building and reaches a rough road. Turn left along this for half a mile. It emerges through the Wye Dale car park onto the A6 main road. Go straight across to the entrance of Topley Pike quarry (still very active) and take a path which at first runs alongside the left side of the quarry road. In a few hundred metres, just beyond a footpath direction sign, go straight ahead up a short side dale; you are now on the alternative route of Walk 16 (if you turned right at the sign you would reach the main route of Walk 16 in a few metres).

The path bears to the right opposite a cave ('Churn Hole') and climbs steeply up the end of the dale to a wooden stile. Follow the wall on your left till it turns away at a footpath signpost, and go straight ahead to join a farm track. Where this turns sharp left go straight ahead over a wooden stile, through the left-hand wall gap and over another stile, passing left of a farmhouse, to join a walled track at a stile beside an iron gate. Where the walls end go straight on, over a step stile just right of a gate, after which the track becomes walled again and you soon reach the road. Go straight across into another walled track; this will bring you to the main street of Chelmorton just below the church.

Walk 18: Pomeroy and Flagg

Start: at SK113682 on the minor road which runs south from Chelmorton to the A515 near Pomeroy, at the bend where it is joined by a green lane (Highstool Lane) running NNE. There is ample room to park on the grass verge near this point, but take care not to obstruct gateways and leave room for farm traffic on the green lane.

Alternatively, park at the roadside in Flagg village, or (if you are a customer) at the Duke of York at Pomeroy.

Distance: 4¼ miles (alternatives 3½ to 4½)

Public transport: there are three or four buses a day (except Sunday) on a circular route from Buxton – Chelmorton – Flagg – Monyash – Pomeroy – Buxton. They pass near the station at Buxton.

On Sundays there are one or two buses a day on the Sheffield – Bakewell – Buxton and Mansfield – Derby – Buxton – Castleton routes, and in summer also one on the Huddersfield – Buxton – Matlock route. These all pass the Duke of York at Pomeroy, and are timed to suit those who want a day out.

Amenities: there are pubs in Flagg, Chelmorton and Monyash (where there are also cafes), besides the Duke of York and others on the A515, and of course many pubs and cafes in Buxton. My favourites are the Plough in Flagg (at the east end of the village) and the Packhorse at Crowdecote, a mile east of Longnor.

There are toilets at the Grin Low picnic site (SK050720) west of Harpur Hill, at the Parsley Hay car park (SK147638) just off the A515, and in Longnor and Buxton.

The walk starts on the park boundary near Pomeroy, 5 miles south-east of Buxton; follows a green road towards Chelmorton; and returns by way of Flagg. The route is mainly through fields, some cultivated but mostly pasture. Flagg is a small strung-out village; Pomeroy just a pub and a couple of farms.

About 200 metres are along quiet byroads and another 100 metres alongside the A515, which is busy but has a grass verge. Most of the route should be firm underfoot (although this depends whether any of the fields has been ploughed recently) but there are a few muddy patches.

The walk is on the 'West' side of the 'White Peak' OS map.

Step stile at Flagg

The Walk

From the starting point on the minor road south of Chelmorton, walk along the green lane (Highstool Lane) for a mile until it meets another minor road (the route of the Monyash Circular bus). Turn right along it for about a hundred metres and go over a step stile on the right (with footpath signpost) just beyond the first cross wall **(1)**. Go diagonally across the field and into the little valley (the more obvious path further right is only a cattle track). This brings you to a step stile under a chestnut tree – it can be muddy here; the firmest way is close to the wall on the right of the stile.

Cross the stile and bear slightly left of the valley bottom, towards a stile directly in line with the spire of Monyash church which you can see in the distance; just before the stile, notice a couple of very small quarries for stone for the wall. Cross the stile and go diagonally across the field towards a small wood, to the left of a farm. A step stile and a gateway just to the right of the wood bring you into a field with some mounds; pass these and bear right, over two step stiles, to reach a minor road at a corner **(2)**. This is Town Head, the west end of Flagg village.

Alternative routes diverge here, but the main route turns left along

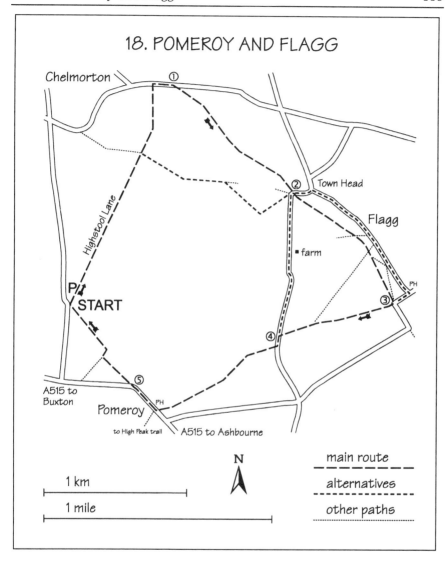

18. POMEROY AND FLAGG

Chelmorton ①

② Town Head

Flagg

■ farm

PH

③

P ↑
START

④

⑤

A515 to
Buxton

Pomeroy PH

to High Peak trail   A515 to Ashbourne

Highstool Lane

N

1 km

1 mile

main route
— — — —
alternatives
- - - - - - - -
other paths
....

the road for a few metres and crosses a step stile on the right, with a
footpath signpost. Turn left and aim for the bottom of the shallow valley,
which runs almost parallel with the village street. Cross two step stiles,
each a few metres to the right of a rather muddy gateway. The next stile
is at the right-hand end of a clump of trees, and the next only a few

metres on, with a patch of mud beyond it. Go on down the valley and over another step stile, and aim left of the isolated tree for the next one.

Here the right of way bends left towards the street and then right again, but if it is not apparent on the ground you should aim to the right of the rightmost houses, a group of semis, and you will find a stile beneath a tree. This brings you to a minor road at a sharp bend **(3)**. Do not follow the road but turn right into a field, then follow the wall on your left for half a mile, over several stiles, till you reach a very quiet road **(4)**. (The OS map shows a path from the middle of Flagg which cuts off a corner, but this crosses a field which is regularly ploughed so may be muddy).

Turn left along the road for a short way and then right over a step stile, with a waymark post. Go up the field with the wall on your right, then through two gates close together where there was once a barn. Now bear rather to the left, passing a tiny pond, to the far corner of the field. Cross a step stile, and another very close to it, and then go up the middle of the field aiming just to the right of a bungalow and electricity pole on the skyline. Cross two more stiles, bearing slightly right, and a third which brings you out on the main A515 road at Pomeroy, by the car park of the Duke of York Inn.

Turn right and walk along the road past the inn (or visit it if you choose, though it is perhaps a bit upmarket for walkers and you are asked to leave your boots and pack at the door). About a hundred metres further on, where the road bears left **(5)**, go straight ahead for a few metres to a footpath signpost. Do not go on between the concrete gateposts, but go over the step stile on the right and turn left alongside the wall.

Go over another step stile and on through a gateway, then turn half-right to a stile hidden behind an electricity post. Turn left alongside the wall again, and continue over three step stiles to arrive back at the beginning of Highstool Lane.

Alternative routes

If you prefer you can walk along the quiet village street at Flagg instead of along the path parallel to it; this will add less than a quarter of a mile to the distance. The street forms part of the 'Limestone Way' long distance path. When you come out at the road corner at Town Head **(2)**, turn left along the road and ignore the stile on the right. You will soon come to a road junction. Turn right along the village street, which is unusual in that practically all the buildings are on the same side of the street. In half a mile, at the end of the street, turn right (if you turn left you will soon reach the Plough Inn). Where the road turns left beyond the last houses **(3)**, go straight ahead into a field and follow the wall on your left; you are now back on the main route.

You can shorten the route by about half a mile (and avoid most of the muddy patches), at the cost of walking for half a mile along a very quiet byroad, if you leave out Flagg village. When you reach the road at Town Head **(2)**, turn right instead of left along the road. After about half a mile, well beyond the farm, look out for a stile and waymark post on each side of the road – first on the left and then on the right **(4)**. Go over the one on the right, and you are back on the main route.

Also you can shorten either this reduced route or the main one by a quarter of a mile (and avoid another muddy patch) if you leave High-stool Lane before its end. About two thirds of a mile from the starting point, beyond two or three small trees, look out for an iron gate and step stile on each side of the track – the one on the right has a signpost. Go over this one, and slightly right, in the direction of the signpost arm, towards the (hidden) far corner of the field.

In the corner you will find a footpath signpost. Go over the step stile just to its right and turn left alongside the wall. Cross a step stile and a ladder stile. Now bear rather to the right as indicated by the signpost arm (this is an official diversion; the original route ran through the farmyard). Go through a wooden squeezer (if it is still there – the fence looks temporary), across a farm track and another wooden squeezer, and on to another pair of squeeezers in a hedge, just right of an old railway van. Now follow the fence on your right past the van, through another squeezer (mind the barbed wire) and on to the road corner where you rejoin the main route, at Town Head **(2)**.

Walk 19: Upper Lathkill Dale

Start: Beside the B5055 Monyash to Bakewell road where it crosses the head
                      of Lathkill Dale, half a mile east of the centre of Monyash (SK 158665).
                      There is room for several cars on the verge, but this spot is popular on
                      summer weekends; if full, park in Monyash village where there is a car
                      park on the road which runs north from the crossroads.

Distance: 3¼ miles (alternatives 4 or 4¼).

Public transport: There are three or four buses each weekday from Buxton to Monyash,
                      about half a mile from the route of the walk. On Mondays only there are
                      morning and afternoon buses from Leek and Bakewell. There is no
                      Sunday service.

Amenities: You can eat at the inn at the crossroads in Monyash, which has resumed
                      its original name of the Bull's Head after a few years as the Hobbit; or at
                      the Plough in Flagg a mile and a half north. There is a very down-to-earth
                      little cafe ('Muddy boots welcome') beside the Bull's Head, and another
                      cafe the other side of the church.

                      There are many inns and cafes in Hartington, Longnor, Bakewell and
                      Buxton, all within a few miles.

                      There are public toilets in Monyash, at the car park on the road signposted
                      to Newhaven and Parsley Hay, but these are apparently not maintained
                      by the Council and are not always in order. However there are toilets at
                      the High Peak Trail car park at Parsley Hay two miles south of Monyash,
                      just across the A515, and at Over Haddon car park.

Lathkill Dale is one of the most beautiful of the dales, and one which
changes its character as you go upstream. It is an open dale with
riverside meadows from Alport to Over Haddon; a steeper, wooded dale
with relics of past mining from here to the ruins of Carter's Mill; open
again, but steeper and with sides largely of rock and scree, and mainly
dry at most seasons, to Ricklow Quarry; and then a narrow rocky defile
for a few hundred metres before it opens out into pastureland as it comes
to the B5055 road. There are many delightful walks, although the main
route along the length of the valley does not lend itself to a short circular
walk.

The route I describe here explores the upper part of the dale. It may
be muddy in places after rain, though boots will cope with it; in fact it

Bull's Head, Monyash

is probably at its most interesting a day or two after a spell of heavy rain, especially in winter. The first quarter mile is along a minor road.

The sketch map is drawn with East at the top.

The Walk

Walk eastwards (away from Monyash) along the road for a quarter of a mile. When the road levels out, look out for a point where the wall on the right steps back a few metres further from the road. Go through a gate on the right just short of this point; go half left through a wall gap, and continue diagonally across the field to where you can see a wooden stile in the far wall. Go over it and continue in the same direction over the brow of the hill, and you will see a signpost just beyond the wall in the valley bottom. Go over the step stile to the left of it **(1)**.

Now turn right, alongside the wall. The signpost does not have an arm pointing this way, but you will shortly pass a waymark and then, at the next stile, a signpost to confirm that you are on a right of way. Continue down Ricklow Dale until you reach a gate, at the beginning of the old quarry workings **(2)**.

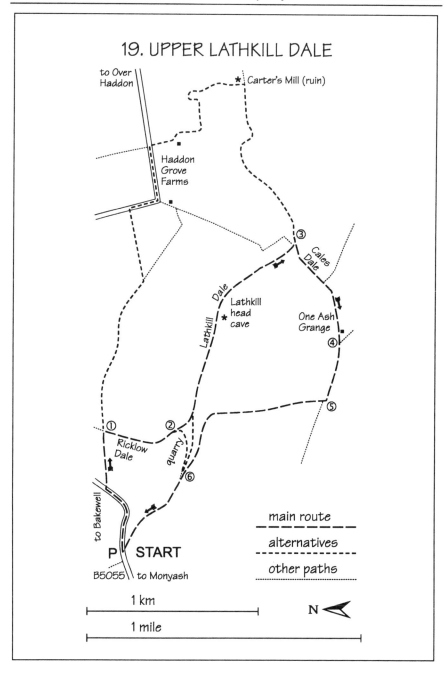

19. UPPER LATHKILL DALE

to Over Haddon

*Carter's Mill (ruin)

Haddon Grove Farms

③

Cales Dale

Lathkill Dale

*Lathkill head cave

One Ash Grange

④

⑤

① Ricklow Dale

②

quarry

⑥

to Bakewell

P START

B5055 \ to Monyash

main route

alternatives

other paths

1 km

1 mile

N

The right of way is through the gate and the stile beyond it, on an obvious path. After passing the end of two very straight waste rock tips on your right, look for a lesser but still clear path which branches right; the main path, which goes on rising, leads only to the upper quarry working. You need to find a way down to the dale bottom. It is not obvious which is the right of way, but the first apparent way down is very steep and rocky; the next is better, and evidently used, but involves a rocky scramble. The last, past a tree, runs diagonally down the hillside, passing just above the last of the tips to meet a wall where it reaches the valley bottom, and this is the easiest way although still steep. Go over the stile and down the valley, Lathkill Dale.

There is an alternative concessionary path which adds about a quarter of a mile but is easier going. It also includes one of the most interesting parts of Lathkill Dale, which the other path misses. It is waymarked (though not generously) and is evidently the way that the owners of this land, which is a nature reserve, would prefer you to use. To go this way, do not go through the gate **(2)** at the beginning of the quarry workings but turn right up the hillside, as indicated by a 'Lathkill Dale' signpost (if it survives; it was somewhat decayed when I last passed it). After a short steep climb over grass and rocks, where the path is not clear, bear rather to the left to follow the fence over the brow of the hill and gently down into Lathkill Dale.

Turn left over the stile and follow the obvious path down the bottom of the dale. It is rocky in places, but not difficult. This upper part of the dale is dry and narrow, with limestone sides which though not high are vertical or even overhanging in places; they grow fine icicles in frosty weather. Shortly Ricklow Dale joins on the left, but it is completely hidden by a rock tip from Ricklow Quarry which reaches right into Lathkill Dale. Beyond the tip you soon come to a stile; the path described previously joins the dale just before the stile.

The dale opens out a little as the sides become less steep and rocky, though higher. In about a quarter of a mile you will come to Lathkill Head cave on the right. In the summer it is usually dry, and the river rises at springs half a mile further down the dale; but in wet weather the stream issues from the cave, and after a few days heavy rain it can be quite spectacular. Lesser streams issue at several other points down this side of the valley. The path crosses here to the left side of the valley; if the stream is running high you may have to backtrack a few metres from the cave to cross.

In another quarter of a mile you will come to a footbridge **(3)**. Cross it, and follow the obvious path up the side dale, Cales Dale. This is usually dry, but in wet weather it carries a stream which issues from a cave just below the path, about a hundred metres up. A little further on the path divides. Look back here to enjoy the view of Lathkill Dale and the rocky crags beyond it. Take the right-hand path, which climbs diagonally up the side of the dale, past a signpost, into a defile with a sheer rock wall on the right and a short mine tunnel on the left, and eventually over a stile into a field.

You can see the buildings of One Ash Grange farm at the end of the field. Keep to the right of most of the buildings but just to the left of a black corrugated iron barn; the path goes up stone steps and over a stile, then on along a track which may be muddy. Notice an arch on the right which leads into a chamber which presumably served as a larder, and a row of pigsties with spouts for pouring swill into the troughs. Where this track meets another, turn right, uphill **(4)**.

The track runs up a very narrow field used mainly as a farm machinery store. At the top of the field it turns right through a gateway and divides **(5)**. The left-hand track, which goes back to the original direction, leads in a mile to Monyash; but unless you want to walk into the village, take the right hand track which leads northwards. It goes through several gateways, and then seems to disappear; but in fact it bears left as a much fainter track, with Lathkill Dale visible over the wall on the right and Ricklow Quarry beyond the dale. The track slopes gently down into the dale, and joins it just beyond the point you reached on the concessionary path from the quarry gate **(6)**. Turn left up the dale, which is only a slight depression here, and you will be back at your starting point in a quarter of a mile.

Alternative routes

To add a mile, start as described but when you reach Ricklow Dale, do not turn right beyond the stile **(1)** but go straight on up the other side of the valley as indicated by the signpost. In half a mile you cross another shallow dale and climb diagonally up the far side to a stile. Beyond it the path runs straight ahead to Haddon Grove farm, but the farmyard is very muddy. So take the path which branches left and runs alongside the wall on your left, across two fields to the road.

Turn right, follow the road round the bend at the farm entrance, and in 300 metres go through a gate on the right and down a walled track, originally the way to Carter's Mill in the dale bottom. The track continues past a farm on the right, and then winds down an attractive side dale to meet Lathkill Dale at the slight remains of the mill, with its dam. Turn right up the dale, which is open on this side though wooded on the other. At the upper end of the millpond is a natural dam of tufa, a material formed when limestone dissolved in the water (which reaches here via an underground cave system) is deposited on moss and weed in the river bed.

A short way above here are the springs where the Lathkill rises when Lathkill Head cave is dry, and in half a mile you will reach the footbridge at the foot of Cales Dale. You can either cross it and follow the main route past One Ash Grange, or shorten the alternative route to 4 miles by continuing straight up the dale bottom to your starting point.

Walk 20: Monyash, Derby Lane and Cales Farm

Start: At the car park (SK150667) in Monyash, on the Flagg road leading north from the crossroads and a short way beyond the telephone box. Alternatively, park carefully in one of the village streets.

Distance: 4 miles (alternative 5)

Public transport: There is no Sunday bus service, but on other days there are four buses a day from Buxton, some running through from New Mills.

Amenities: The Bull's Head (for a few years the Hobbit) at the crossroads in Monyash serves bar meals. The cosy little cafe beside it positively welcomes muddy boots (and serves tea by the pint) and is evidently a favourite with walkers and cyclists. There is another cafe beyond the church.

Although there are toilets signposted in Monyash (at a former garage, in front of an agricultural merchants, just before the pond on the road leading south towards Newhaven), these are apparently not maintained by the council and have been out of order on some of my visits to the village. However there are toilets at the Parsley Hay car park a mile and a half south, and in Youlgreave and Bakewell.

The first part of the walk follows Derby Lane, in medieval times part of a through route from Manchester to Derby and still legally a public highway, although part of it is now only an unmarked footpath across fields. It returns past Cales Farm (with an alternative descending into Lathkill Dale), and joins the Limestone Way long-distance path for the last half mile. Apart from this last stage it is little used and you may not meet another walker.

Most of the walk is along firm paths and it is suitable for most weathers; in places there may be shallow mud over the firm surface, but boots should cope.

The Walk

Walk to the village crossroads and straight across, into the Parsley Hay and Newhaven road. Pass the pond and continue to the end of the village. The road turns right here, but your way is straight ahead for a few metres to a 'Limestone Way' waymark post **(1)**. Do not take the way it indicates (you will return that way) but turn right along a tarmac lane. This is Derby Lane and was in medieval times part of a through route,

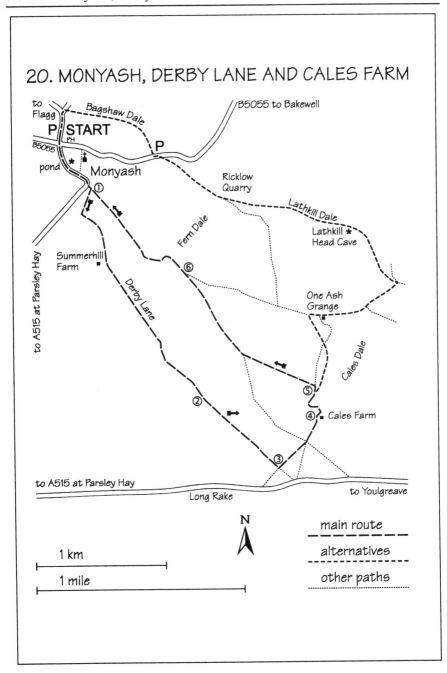

20. MONYASH, DERBY LANE AND CALES FARM

though now it carries no traffic except the occasional farm vehicle. (I am indebted to Mike Cresswell's 'Walking Peakland Trackways' for making me aware of this route).

Beyond the farm the tarmac ends but a firm walled track continues for nearly a mile. Near where it swings right by a small wood, look out on the left for an old guidestone which now does duty as a gatepost (SK156651). Eventually the walled track ends at a cross wall (2). The right of way continues, though unmarked, through the gate ahead and follows the wall on your left.

Follow the wall across a little valley (the head of Cales Dale) and up to a gate. Now the right of way is diagonally across a large field, to reach the road at the same point as a farm drive. However, half way across the field (3) you cross (invisibly) another right of way, running down the bottom of a little valley, and you should turn left along this. It leads through a gateway, and at the next gateway it joins a farm track. Go on along this, but at the next gateway (4) do not go through into Cales Farm farmyard but bear left along the track signed 'One Ash Grange'.

The path descends into a shallow dale (Cales Dale again) and climbs the other side, and after levelling out comes to a cattle grid (5). For the main walk do not cross the grid, but turn left immediately before it and follow the wall on your right. Towards the end of the long field are small quarries on the left, a good spot for spring flowers, and on the right a view of the rocky sides of Lathkill Dale: One Ash Grange farm is hidden in the dip in between.

Go over a step stile and bear slightly right to the far corner of the field, just beyond a dip. I understand that the path has been waymarked, and some poor stiles improved, since I passed. Beside a footpath sign which had lost its arm is a stile: cross it and then turn rather more than half left across the field, making for a village and a hill on the skyline with a steep drop on its left – if it isn't clear enough to see so far, walk roughly parallel to the power cables away on your left. Go through a gap in the derelict wall and then on to a step stile on the skyline. At this point, one March, we watched three hares boxing each other – hence the expression 'Mad as a March Hare', no doubt.

Go on in the same direction across a large field. As you come over the skyline you will see Monyash ahead, with the tip of the spire showing over the trees. Beyond a ruined wall, make for a squeezer and waymark post in the bottom corner of the field (6). From here to Monyash you will be following the 'Limestone Way' long-distance footpath, and the way is clear on the ground. It leads you across a little

Monyash

dale (Fern Dale) to a step stile and footpath signpost. Cross the stile and turn left alongside the wall, and another stile will soon take you into a walled path. This brings you back to Monyash village in about half a mile.

Alternative routes

If you are not already familiar with the upper end of Lathkill Dale, you have the opportunity to include it in your walk at the cost of an extra mile. To do this, at the cattle grid **(5)** after crossing Cales Dale do not turn left, but go straight ahead along the farm track to One Ash Grange. Although the right of way does not follow the track exactly, the track is now marked as a concessionary path and is to be preferred because it avoids the farmyard. At the farm you come to a cross track; go over it and along a signposted level track, between the main farm on the right and smaller buildings on the left. Go just to the right of an iron barn, where you will find a squeezer stile. Follow the bottom of the little valley to a stile and descend steeply into Cales Dale, which is a good deal more spectacular here than where you crossed it before.

At a footpath signpost, ignore the path descending steeply on the right and continue ahead along a path which leads down the dale and into

Lathkill Dale, and turn left along the obvious path beyond the bridge. This leads you up the dale, whose sides gradually become lower. On your left you pass Lathkill Head cave. In wet weather the river emerges in full force from this cave, but in summer this section of the dale is dry. As the dale narrows there is a rough stretch over waste rock from the defunct Ricklow Dale quarry, then a narrow defile leading into a pleasant meadow and on to the road. You can turn left along this into the village, and then right at the crossroads to the car park; but for a quieter walk, only slightly longer, take the path almost opposite. This leads up the dale (here Bagshaw Dale) behind the village to join the Flagg road. Turn left along it for the car park.

The wooded middle part of Lathkill Dale is very attractive; but as it is well known, and described in many other books, I shall not describe it here.

Walk 21: Youlgreave and Conksbury Bridge

Start: At the crossroads (SK212643) by the church in Youlgreave. Do not park in the main street, which is narrow and a bus route. On weekdays you can often find a space in one of the side roads, such as the one leading north from the church, but take care not to obstruct entrances. Parking is harder at weekends; there is usually space in the public car park at the west end of the village, but this will add half a mile to your walk.

It is not easy to park anywhere else on the route (apart from a small layby where the route crosses Back Lane at SK204651), but there is usually space in the car park in Over Haddon village (SK203665). This will add about half a mile to your walk, including a steep descent and ascent.

Distance: 4 miles (alternatives 3½ to 4¼)

Public transport: There is a regular Monday to Saturday bus service (about one an hour) on weekdays to Youlgreave from Bakewell, where it connects with services from most of the towns and cities around the Peak District. There is no Sunday service.

There is a bus approximately every two hours from Bakewell to Over Haddon, but no Sunday service.

On summer Sundays and bank holiday Mondays, a morning bus from Sheffield via Bakewell to Castleton calls at Youlgreave, returning in late afternoon.

Amenities: There are several pubs which suppply food in Youlgreave – the George, the Bull's Head and the Farmyard Inn – and also cafes. There is one pub in Over Haddon, and many pubs and cafes in Bakewell.

There are public toilets opposite the village hall in Youlgreave, down a lane (signposted) which leaves the main street at a telephone box about 300 metres west of the church. There are also toilets at the car park in Over Haddon, though this is a quarter of a mile and a stiff climb from the route of the walk.

This walk starts in Youlgreave, three miles south of Bakewell, and crosses the fields to reach Lathkill Dale below Over Haddon. It then follows the Lathkill to the confluence of the river Bradford, and up this river back to Youlgreave.

Lathkill Dale is one of the most attractive dales, with contrasting scenery in its upper and middle reaches and in the lower section explored here. It can be quite busy at weekends, though quieter during

Footbridge over River Bradford at Youlgreave

the week. The route from Youlgreave to the dale is less well used, partly because it is not obvious from the OS map that the path between Meadow Place Grange and Over Haddon is in fact a right of way.

The route described is mostly firm underfoot; but there are two short stretches near Meadow Place Grange which are muddy, so your boots will probably need cleaning after the walk. There is very little road walking.

Youlgreave is one of the larger Peak District villages, with several shops and pubs and some very attractive corners. The church is impressive, and the circular stone conduit house dated 1826, once the source of water for the village, with the cottages nearby makes an attractive scene. The village lies close to the river Bradford but the river cannot be seen from the main street, though several lanes and paths lead down to it.

The Walk

From Youlgreave church, walk westward along the village street for about 200 metres to the round stone conduit house, in front of the post office **(1)**. Fork right here, and continue up Moor Lane which climbs steeply out of the village. Beyond the last houses it bends right and then left. Immediately past this second bend, fork right onto a walled track; the footpath sign here had lost its arm when I passed. The track is mainly firm though there may be mud in places.

Where the track ends, go straight ahead through a squeezer beside a gate and on with the wall on your left. The way ahead is obvious (although the OS map shows a slightly different line); over a wooden stile in a wire fence, across a little valley, and up to a squeezer stile about 50 metres right of the field corner. Another squeezer a few metres on **(2)** brings you onto a tarmac road (Back Lane). Go a few metres right,

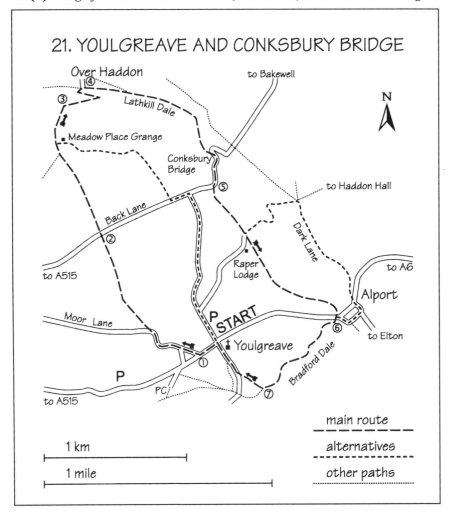

21. YOULGREAVE AND CONKSBURY BRIDGE

main route

alternatives

other paths

1 km

1 mile

then left over a stone stile, signposted 'Over Haddon', and across the field with the wall on your right. As you approach a large farm, Meadow Place Grange, you will see a gate a little to your left at the bottom of the field.

A short but usually muddy walled track leads into the large farmyard, with an impressive range of stone buildings – one is dated 1850. Your way is straight across into a similar short muddy track between farm buildings (waymarked). A gate leads into a field and you go straight across it, bearing slightly right towards the houses which soon come in sight, to a wooden gate **(3)**. Here you are on the edge of a wooded section of Lathkill Dale, with the village of Over Haddon on the opposite edge.

Go through the gate and down a firm track through trees (a right of way, although this is not obvious from the OS map). This doubles back on itself to reach the dale bottom at a ford **(4)** – though the river here is usually dry. A stone slab footbridge (with some impressive fossils, though rather spoilt by an ugly handrail) is provided in case you need it. The lane straight ahead leads quickly but steeply into Over Haddon, but your route is to the right. The path rounds a garden and continues with the river bed on the right. It is firm underfoot, but where it rises over some rocks these can be slippery if wet. At some point (just where depends on the season and weather) the river emerges from its bed, and a series of low weirs form calm ponds, popular with water birds, all along the next stretch.

In rather more than half a mile you reach the attractive old Conksbury Bridge. Turn right along the road, over the bridge, and in about 200 metres **(5)** turn left onto a firm footpath (signpost missing). Here the valley opens out and the path is less close to the river. In a quarter of a mile it reaches a lane, and on the right is a stone house with 'Gothick' pointed windows – this is Raper Lodge, which was recently used as a film setting. There is a choice of ways here, but the main route continues straight ahead across the meadows, with the Lathkill on the left, till it reaches the road at Alport **(6)**.

Your route is straight across the road and down a drive beside a telephone box and a welcome seat, but if you have time and energy you may like to walk down the byroad slightly further left to look at the pleasant hamlet of Alport with its hump-backed bridge and old mill. Look out for a curious building with classical pillars some way off the road on the left. Return to this point, and follow the drive to a stile beside a white gate. Just before this you cross the river Bradford, though it is so small that you could easily miss it. The Lathkill and the Bradford are amongst the clearest streams in the country, and both seem to have alternative routes underground so that the surface flow may be very modest in places.

Follw the riverside path round an impressive rock, best seen by looking back after you pass it. The path joins a track, and you can save a few metres by cutting across the bend to a hump-backed stone footbridge **(7)**. Cross this and walk up the steep footpath to the road. Turn right, and you will be back at the church in a few hundred metres.

Alternative routes

You can shorten the walk by half a mile by turning right at Raper Lodge, up a narrow lane which brings you out in Youlgreave. Turn left at the top to return to the church.

The worse of the two muddy sections at Meadow Place Grange can be avoided if you leave Youlgreave by the road running north from the church, by the George Inn, instead of by Moor Lane and the path across the fields. In half a mile you reach a T junction; turn left, and in about 100 metres turn right into a farm road. This brings you into the yard of Meadow Place Grange in half a mile (the road is a public highway, although this is not obvious from the OS map). Go through a waymarked gap in the farm buildings on your right (not close to the farmhouse) and you are back on the main route. The distance is little different.

If you wish you can add a quarter mile by turning left at Raper Lodge. The bridle track (signposted 'Haddon Hall') leads over a pleasant stone footbridge and zigzags steeply up through a wood. At the top, go through an iron gate and turn right (as waymarked) alongside the fence. Where the fence ends, just before a barn, go through the iron gate on the right (or over it if padlocked). Go down the lane (Dark Lane), which is tarmac although the first few metres may be covered in mud. This again is a public highway though not marked as such. After a level stretch, from which you can see the wooded lower valley of the Lathkill to your left, the lane drops through trees to meet a road at Alport. The telephone box and the main route are a hundred metres to your right along this road, although you may prefer to cross it and take the loop road through the village – if so, keep right at the road junction and do not cross either the road bridge or the footbridge.

The section of Lathkill Dale above that explored here is wooded and attractive, and also interesting to naturalists and industrial archaeologists. However it is well covered by other guidebooks, and especially by a booklet published by the Peak Park Planning Board. Beyond this, the upper part of the dale is explored in walk 19.

Walk 22: Bradford Dale and Harthill Moor

Start: Youlgreave car park, SK205641. This is at the west end of the village street, just beyond the last house, on the road which leads to Middleton and Newhaven; it is about half a mile from the church.

It is unwise to park in the main street of the village, since this is narrow and is a bus route. One or two cars can park by the bridge over the Bradford, or in the side road which runs north from the church (not on your route unless you decide to visit the church), but these spaces will be full at summer weekends.

Distance: 3½ miles (though it feels further!): alternatives 2½ to 5 miles.

Public transport: There is an hourly bus from Bakewell to Youlgreave, Monday to Saturday. On Sundays, two buses a day from Bakewell to Buxton and beyond run via Youlgreave, and one or both come through from Sheffield.

Bakewell is well served by buses from many towns around the Peak District.

Amenities: Youlgreave has several inns which provide hot food. There are also cafes, including a popular one hidden away near the village hall.

There are toilets at the village hall, which is down a narrow street (signposted) off the main street about 200 metres west of the church. There are also toilets in the car park, but these are more basic and may be locked.

The walk starts from the village of Youlgreave, drops into Bradford Dale and then climbs past Hopping Farm to Harthill Moor. It returns along the route of the 'Limestone Way' footpath. An optional extension takes in Robin Hood's Stride, an imposing rocky outcrop, and the 'Hermit's Cave'.

Youlgreave is a large pleasant village, though not one much visited by tourists except at well-dressing time in late June. It stretches for over half a mile along its main street, with several attractive lanes leading off it. The church, with its massive tower, is one of the finest in the Peak District. Bradford Dale runs parallel with the main street and quite close to it, although houses hide it from view.

The river Bradford, like the Lathkill which it joins, is one of the clearest rivers in the country. It has many weirs to create pools for

Robin Hood's Stride

fishing, and to drive long-gone watermills. At Youlgreave it runs in a steep wooded dale.

The walk is partly on the limestone through which Bradford Dale is cut, and partly on the gritstone of Harthill Moor; the colour of the walls will give you the clue. About half a mile is along a minor road or the village street. Much of the rest is firm underfoot, but there may be some mud after rain.

The Walk

Turn right (away from the village) as you leave the car park. In about 100 metres, just beyond a seat, take a footpath (with FP signpost) on the left. This leads gently down through the trees into Bradford Dale, and then alongside the river Bradford. The flow is small (and the river may be completely dry a little further up), but weirs hold it back to make wide calm pools.

Beyond a step stile and a squeezer the path joins a track. Turn left along it over the bridge, and then right, passing two dry millponds. Nothing now remains of the corn mills which once served Youlgreave

22. BRADFORD DALE AND HARTHILL MOOR

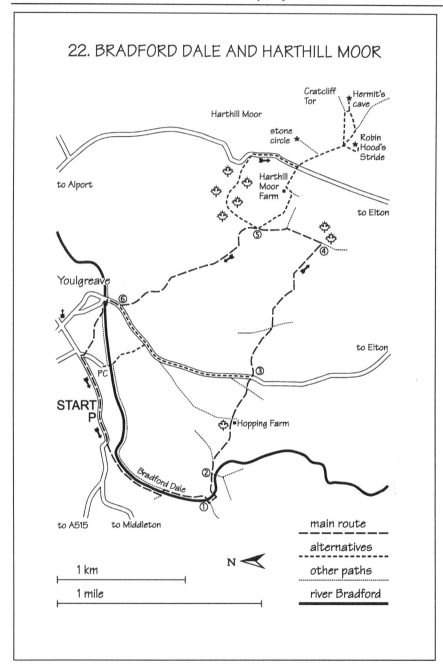

and Middleton. The path swings to the right, across the dale, and then forks **(1)**. Take the left fork, which continues up a rocky section of the dale. Beyond a footbridge the path climbs the dale side by an iron staircase, then turns right along the dale rim.

Shortly the dale opens out into a wide basin, with Smerril Grange in sight ahead of you. Where the path descends to stream level there is a stone slab bridge on your right **(2)**. Do not cross it, but follow the path which curves left into a side valley. (This path breaks into several parallel strands; choose the lowest unless it is too muddy).

You can now see a squeezer stile ahead and another higher up to your left. Take the right-hand one, near a double electricity pole, and continue up the hill; aim just right of a clump of trees which partly stands on a mound. Soon you will come to a stile and see Hopping Farm ahead of you, and in summer also many tents and caravans (the site belongs to the Camping Club).

Go through the squeezer at the gate by the left end of the farmhouse, and pass between the house and an outbuilding to another squeezer beside an ornate iron gate, then straight across the farm track and through yet another squeezer – a signpost indicates that the path goes to Robin Hood's Stride. Go straight up the field (which may be full of tents), with the hedge on your left, to a squeezer at the top. Beyond this a short fenced path takes you to another squeezer. Go through it and turn right up the hill, with the wall on your right. From this point there is a fine view back across the valley to Youlgreave.

Cross the sunken road by a pair of stiles **(3)** and go almost straight ahead to an inconspicuous step stile, and on up the hill to another on the hilltop. Now go straight across a large field, dropping slightly, to a squeezer almost in line with the right-hand end of a wood. Carry on towards a gateway, and you will find a footpath signpost and stile just to its right. Go straight on over the stile and on to a gateway in the middle of the opposite wall. From here go half right, diagonally across the field, to a squeezer, and on in the same direction to a wooden stile in a stone wall. Beyond this head towards the farm you can see ahead (Harthill Moor farm) with the wall on your right until you reach a signpost and stile, by which you cross the wall.

You are now in a very large field (a wall shown on the OS map has gone), and your way is diagonally across it towards the right-hand edge of a small wood, where there is a stile and footpath sign **(4)**. Do not cross the stile, but turn your back on it and head back across the field, following the power lines, to a stile not far from its lowest point. (The direct route from the previous stile, straight down alongside the wall, is not a right of way). The stile leads to a farm track; go straight ahead down it. Beyond a gate there is a pair of footpath signposts **(5)** telling you that you have reached the Limestone Way. Fork left along the farm track. From here you will be following the Limestone Way back to Youlgreave; but its waymarking is inadequate, so read on.

The track curves round a spur and then drops to a gateway in a ruined wall. Here turn right, and aim a little left of the tower of Youlgreave church. You will find the next stile just to the left of two tree stumps. Go on to another stile, where you cross a small stream – the path here is partly paved – and on up the hill, aiming straight for the church. Beyond a waymarked stile beside a wooden gate, follow the wall to a squeezer beside another gateway. Go on towards the nearest houses. About two thirds of the way to them you will find a squeezer in the wall on your right. Go through it and aim towards the rightmost pair of houses, where a stile will bring you onto the road **(6)**.

Turn right along the road, and cross the river by either the road bridge or the picturesque slab bridge just upstream. Now turn left through the stile (unless you want to visit the village centre, with its very fine church and several pubs) and follow the riverside path upstream for a hundred metres. Then take a tarmac path which slopes up the dale side on your right. This crosses a stile and becomes a minor road. Where it joins the village street there is a fine 17th century house in front of you, and the village hall, toilets, and a cafe are down the lane to the left.

Turn half left along the main street of the village, and you will be back at the car park in a third of a mile.

Alternative routes

You can add a mile and a half by making an excursion to Robin Hood's Stride and Cratcliff Tor, with its hermit's cave. The Stride is a rocky outcrop with two pillars of rock which give the impression (if it's misty, or you have plenty of imagination) of the chimneys of a mansion; hence its alternative name of 'Mock Beggar's Hall'. It is a good viewpoint.

To do this, follow the main walk till you join the Limestone Way below Harthill Moor farm **(5)**. Go through the wicket gate on your right and bear left, along the Limestone Way, which follows the contours and curves through a wood to reach a minor road. Turn right along it, and after less than a quarter mile turn left opposite the farm entrance on a signposted path which aims for the rocks. The path is clear, going over a step stile just left of a gateway and crossing another stile beside a gate, from where you scramble up to the Stride by a path which climbs round its right-hand side.

Return to the path by the last stile and go straight across through a wall gap, and along the ridge with a wood on your right. Go through a stile and immediately turn right (or go ahead for a short way to enjoy the view from Cratcliff Tor, and return to this point). Ignore a wooden stile on the right and bear left round the foot of the rocks till you reach a large yew tree, behind which is the hermit's cave. It is guarded by an ugly iron railing, but through it you can see a carving of Christ crucified on the right-hand wall. Holes and slots in the rock above the cave suggest extensions which must have made the hermit quite comfortable. It is said that a nineteenth century landowner supported a 'hermit' as a tourist attraction, although it seems that a genuine hermit was here in the 14th century and the carving may date from that time.

You may like to go a few metres further to see some spectacular rocky cliffs (don't fail to look above your head!), but then return to the wooden stile and this time cross it and follow a path through the trees to a stone stile. Turn right, through an iron gate, past the Stride and back to the road by the same path.

From the field nearest the road you can walk to a group of standing stones which are all that remain of a small prehistoric stone circle. This, the cave and the Stride are all off the right of way but they are very frequently visited without objection.

You can return to the wicket gate by the way you came, through the wood, and this would be wise after rain. But for a shorter, though possibly muddy, route go straight across and along the farm drive. Follow the track to the left in front of the farmhouse and then take the right fork. From here the right of way is very clearly waymarked, though muddy at first. It keeps near the wall on the right, without crossing it, until you reach a steeply sloping field and here the way is diagonally down the slope, towards the wicket gate which you will soon see down in the dip. Go through it and turn right along the main route.

For a shorter walk (2½ miles); when you reach the road beyond Hopping Farm (**3**), turn left along it. In about half a mile the road bears right at the entrance to Hopping Farm. If you want to look at Youlgreave village, stay on the road; this is joined, at the houses, by the main route. Otherwise turn left over a stile in a hundred metres. The path takes you into the dale and across a footbridge. Take the alley which bears left, or the road which bears right if you want the cafe or toilets. Either way you will reach the village street; turn left for the car park.

Walk 23: Mill Close and Stanton Moor

Start: In Birchover village, where Uppertown Lane ('Unfit for motors') leaves the main village street on its south side (SK239622). Park at the kerbside; the road is quiet and reasonably wide.

Alternatively, park half a mile further north-east on the Stanton Lees road, at a point where there is a National Trust sign ('Stanton Moor Edge') and a pair of stone gateposts set back on the left of the road (SK247625). There is room for three or four cars, but the space may be full at summer weekends. Parking in Stanton Lees is not recommended because the roads are narrow.

Distance: 4½ miles (alternatives 3½ to 4½).

Public transport: There are about six buses a day, except Sunday, on a roundabout route between Matlock bus station (which is near the railway station, on the branch line from Derby) and Bakewell. These buses stop close to the starting point in Birchover. There is no Sunday service. However the walk passes about a mile from Darley Dale where there is a frequent service along the A6.

Amenities: There are two pubs in Birchover, the Druid and the Red Lion (both towards the west end of the village), and I understand that both provide food although I have not sampled either. The village shop offers ices and cold drinks. There are many pubs and cafes in Bakewell and Matlock.

There are public toilets in Birchover, a short way west of the starting point.

The walk starts in the village of Birchover four miles north-west of Matlock, descends gently through woodland to the old lead mining area of Mill Close, and climbs through the tiny village of Stanton Lees to return across Stanton Moor.

You will pass a small prehistoric stone circle; memorials from the 19th century; and evidence of lead mining, old and new. There is a pleasant woodland stretch and a return across the high, heather-covered Stanton Moor which forms an island of gritstone in the mainly lime-stone area of the White Peak. There are also views into the Derwent Valley, though this part of it is extensively built up and therefore excluded from the National Park.

Although most of Stanton Moor is unfenced, you should keep to the clear paths (in any case the heather makes it hard going away from

Nine Ladies Stone Circle, Stanton Moor

them). A three quarter mile stretch of the steep eastern slope of the moor belongs to the National Trust, and has two good paths through it which are used for some of the 'alternative routes'.

The walk is almost entirely on firm paths (apart from the first woodland section, which can be avoided) and so is suitable for most weather conditions. About a mile and a half is along quiet country roads.

The Walk

Walk down Uppertown Lane, past the recreation ground and on up the hill. At a group of stone buildings, take the roughly metalled lane (Clough Lane) on the left. This is another 'unclassified county road' which is theoretically open to all traffic (I don't recommend driving it if you value your car) and so not signed or mapped as a right of way. The lane winds behind the farm and shortly reaches another farm, where it bends left just beyond the house and continues as a rough but firm walled track. After it crosses the Winster footpath the walls are replaced by verdant banks.

About a quarter of a mile past that footpath, you will see an iron gate in front of you. The lane slips by it on the right. A few metres beyond

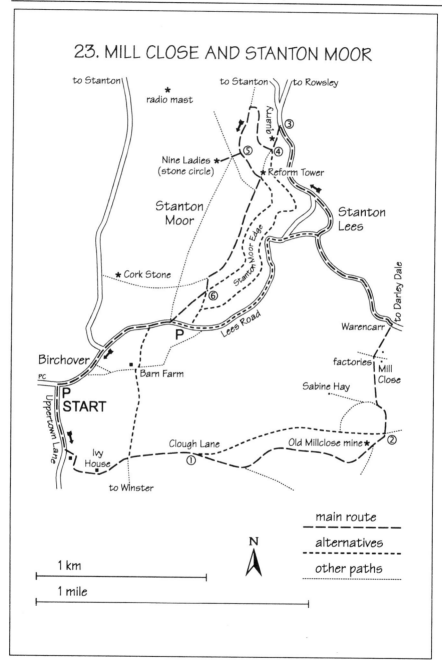

23. MILL CLOSE AND STANTON MOOR

to Stanton

★ radio mast

to Stanton   to Rowsley

③

quarry

Nine Ladies ★
(stone circle)   ⑤   ④

★ Reform Tower

Stanton
Moor

Stanton
Lees

Stanton Moor Edge

★ Cork Stone

⑥

to Darley Dale

Lees Road   Warencarr

P

Birchover   factories   Mill
PC   Barn Farm   Close

P   Sabine Hay
START

Uppertown Lane

Ivy   Clough Lane   Old Millclose mine ★   ②
House   ①

to Winster

main route
‑ ‑ ‑ ‑ ‑ ‑ ‑

alternatives
· · · · · · · · · ·

other paths
· · · · · · · · · ·

N
▲

1 km

1 mile

this, cross a stone stile on the right **(1)**. (The next section of the path may have slippery stretches in wet weather; if so, just continue along the lane – the distance is much the same. At a junction of tracks **(2)**, turn left into the one with a green gate marked 'Sabine Hay').

The path bears left, but keeps well to the right of an overgrown little valley. Shortly it forks. Take the left-hand path, which soon becomes a clear green track sloping gently downhill. Beyond a stile it enters woodland, and shortly crosses a stream (often dry) and continues down the other side of the valley through attractive mixed woodland. You will notice that some of the trees have several slender trunks growing out of a thick stump – they have been coppiced (cut down almost to ground level and allowed to grow again) in the past, probably to be turned into charcoal. The wood is full of flowers in spring.

After rather more than half a mile you come unexpectedly to an imposing ruin on the left of the path. This is the engine house of the Old Millclose Mine, first opened in 1748 and re-opened, as the Watts Shaft, in 1859. The shaft itself is under a concrete cap immediately in front of the building. This is only one of many old mineshafts in the area, a few of which have not been capped, so take care not to stray from the path.

A hundred metres or so further on you come to an iron gate, and beyond this a junction of tracks **(2)**. Turn left, and then right onto a level track with a green gate signed 'Sabine Hay'. On your right you will see the extensive modern buildings of the Mill Close lead smelting plant (you will have been able to hear it for some time). This is on the site of the Mill Close mine, which in the early years of this century was much the most productive in Britain. However it was irretrievably flooded in the 1930s; but the smelter continues using material brought from elsewhere.

In about 150 metres the track passes through a pair of old stone gateposts; here leave the track to take a very straight footpath which slopes downhill to the right, with the remains of well-worn paving. Passing between the lead smelter and other industrial buildings it becomes a tarmac track which leads you to the road at Warrencarr – no more than a few houses.

Turn left along the road, which is not busy except perhaps at the factory closing time. It climbs steeply to the little village of Stanton Lees. At the road junction go straight on (if you want to cut the walk short, turn left and follow the lane for a mile and a half back to Birchover). In about half a mile, go up a track which doubles back on the left **(3)**, with a sign telling you that this is a concessionary path by courtesy of the Haddon estate.

The path shortly comes to an old quarry. Do not enter it, but follow the path to the left of a ruined building. In a few hundred metres there is a junction of paths **(4)**. The one ahead has a National Trust sign, and is described under 'alternative routes'. However the main route turns right and zigzags up the hill, passing more quarries including one with a remarkably sheer rock face. Presumably the names and dates half-way up were cut by climbers.

As the path curves south again and levels out you may notice a path leading to an angular rock at the cliff edge just to your left. If you look at the far side of the rock you will find the inscription 'Y 1826' with a finely carved coronet above. This is one of several such carvings said to exist along the edge, and once visible from the valley although now almost smothered by vegetation – although I've not managed to find all the others. They were the work of the family at the nearby Stanton Hall, which owned the land, and 'Y' is said to stand for the Duke of York.

Beyond this point the path runs alongside Stanton Moor, which is here lightly wooded, but separated from it by a wire fence on your right. When you reach a stile **(5)**, cross it to make a short diversion to look at the Nine Ladies stone circle, about 50 metres ahead – it used to be difficult to find in the trees, but these have now been cleared and a surrounding wall removed to give a better idea of conditions when the circle was built in about 1500 BC. The stones and the circle itself are not large, but on our last visit had attracted a group of (presumably) New Age travellers. A tenth stone, of a different type of rock, lies flat, and a few metres away is the isolated King Stone. There is also an inconspicuous plaque telling you more about the circle.

Return across the stile (though if you want to shorten the walk slightly you can turn right along the clear path you cross on the way) and turn right along your original path. In another few hundred metres you will come to a stone chimney-like tower with a blocked doorway. This is the Reform Tower. It was erected, again by the Thornhill family of Stanton Hall, to commemorate the passing of the Reform Bill in 1832 by Earl Grey; a measure which went a long way towards turning Britain into a modern democracy. A plaque above the door recording this has now gone, along with most of the battlements, and the tower itself is greatly in need of renovation.

The path ahead passes a National Trust sign and continues along the edge of the moor to Birchover (see 'alternative routes'); but at this point

I suggest you cross the stile on the right to enjoy the open moorland, here mostly heather with a few small birch trees and rhododendrons. The path is obvious. Where it branches, any route will take you back to Birchover; but I suggest you take the second branch on the left, which leads over a stile **(6)** and past a National Trust sign to a rocky tor with a fine view down the (rather industrialised) Derwent valley. Then return to the stile. If you parked at the NT sign on the Stanton Lees road, turn left before the stile and follow the path to your car. Otherwise cross the stile and then turn left. In a quarter of a mile you will reach the road. Turn right along it, keeping straight ahead at the road junction, to return to Birchover in less than half a mile.

Alternative routes

I have already suggested a short cut, along the road from Stanton Lees, which reduces the walk to about 3½ miles.

Two pleasant alternative routes use the clear firm paths through the National Trust's Stanton Moor Edge property. For the first, when you have passed the quarry and reached the National Trust sign **(4)**, go straight on past the sign. The path follows the lower edge of the NT property, and cannot be missed. At first it runs through trees but later is more open, with a good view. After three-quarters of a mile it passes below a rocky tor and meets a cross path, with a fence beyond; turn left and you will reach the road in about a hundred metres, at the National Trust sign. Unless you parked here, turn right and you will reach your starting point at Birchover in about half a mile. This route saves perhaps half a mile, but misses out the top of Stanton Moor and its various antiquities.

Another route through the National Trust land from the Reform Tower makes little difference to the distance. Instead of crossing the stile above the tower, take the path past the NT sign which leads along the top edge of the slope with a fence on your right. In a few hunded metres the fence and the path turn right. At this point you can make a short diversion along a path straight ahead, to a large boulder with the cryptic inscription 'EIN 1831' on one side and footholds – now too worn to be safe – leading up the other side. From here there is a fine view across the Derwent valley to the moors beyond. In another half mile or so you will come to a stile on your right **(6)** and a rocky tor on your left, and you are back on the main route. This alternative has better views than the main route, and the advantage that there is only a single path so you cannot go astray.

Yet another possible route from the NT sign at point **(4)**, for the energetic only, is a faint rough path which leads steeply up the hillside between the main route and the level path through the NT property. This brings you directly to the Reform Tower, saving half a mile but missing out the Nine Ladies Stone Circle.

If you parked at the NT sign on the Stanton Lees road, you can reduce the distance by about half a mile if you leave out Birchover village at the start of the walk. Walk towards the village for two or three hundred metres and take a signposted path on the left which leads to Barn Farm (and a small caravan site). Pass through the farm buildings and look out for the Winster footpath on the left. This takes you up the fields for about a third of a mile to join the walled track, Clough Lane, east of Ivy House Farm. Turn left along the track, on the main route.

Stanton Moor has more paths on the ground than I can show on the sketch map: a prominent one is the route of a horse-drawn railway used for timber extraction during the 1914-18 war. If you take any route other than the ones I describe it is important that you realise which road you reach at the far side of the moor. If you descend to the left and reach a winding road part-way down the slope, turn right for Birchover; if you keep up on the moor and come to a level straight road with a white centreline (probably passing the 'Cork Stone', a tall isolated boulder with handholds up the side) you should turn left, then right at the junction, for Birchover.

Walk 24: Friden, Long Dale and Mount Pleasant

Start: At the High Peak Trail car park at Friden (SK172607). The entrance is almost opposite a large factory, on a minor road which runs north towards Youlgreave from the A5012 close to its junction with the A515 Buxton to Ashbourne road at Newhaven. Alternatively there are one or two places where you can park safely on the verge of this minor road, about half a mile further north: this will save you about half a mile of walking.

If you intend to use either of the alternative routes you can park in Middleton-by-Youlgreave (SK196631). There is a small car park just below the recreation ground in the village centre, or you can park carefully at the kerbside.

Distance: 4½ miles (alternatives 3 and 6 miles)

Public transport: Limited, apart from school buses. On Saturdays there are three buses a day on between Ashbourne and Hartington which pass the Newhaven Inn about half a mile from the route, and on Sundays all the year there are two buses each way on the Sheffield to Buxton route which pass the start of the walk, connecting at Buxton with the train service from Manchester and with other buses. On summer Sundays there is also a bus from Huddersfield to Buxton, timed to give a day out, which passes the Newhaven Inn.

There are about 6 buses a day (except Sunday) from Bakewell to Middleton-by-Youlgreave, which is about half a mile from the main route and on both the alternative routes.

Amenities: the Newhaven Inn and the Jug and Glass, on the A515 not far from the start of this walk, are both closed at the time of writing. The restaurant next to the filling station at the Newhaven junction does not appear to open at lunchtime. However there are several pubs and cafes in Hartington, Youlgreave and Bakewell.

There are picnic tables at the Friden car park, and also seats and a picnic table in Middleton-by-Youlgreave.

There are public toilets in Middleton-by-Youlgreave, just below the playground; in Youlgreave near the village hall; and at the car park at Hartington Station (on the road from Hartington to the A515). The Friden car park does not have toilets.

There is good but little-known walking country in the area east of the

Middleton-by-Youlgreave

High Peak Trail, and this route takes you through some of it; you will probably have the paths to yourself. This walk is not too much affected by the weather. There is about a mile of road walking, though you can avoid half of this if you park at the roadside rather than at the Friden car park.

The sketch map is drawn with East at the top.

The Walk

Walk down to the car park entrance, turn right under the bridge and follow the road for about a quarter of a mile. Just before the bottom of the dip **(1)**, take a path which forks right and turns right through a gate to follow a walled track along the bottom of the valley, which is called Long Dale. (The first part of this track is missing from some OS maps, but it is obvious on the ground and is a right of way). In May the field on the right is full of cowslips. Where the walled lane ends, an obvious track continues along the valley bottom. At the end of the woods, keep to the track as it slants up the left side of the valley, among scattered rocks with more cowslips and a few orchids.

24. FRIDEN, LONG DALE AND MOUNT PLEASANT

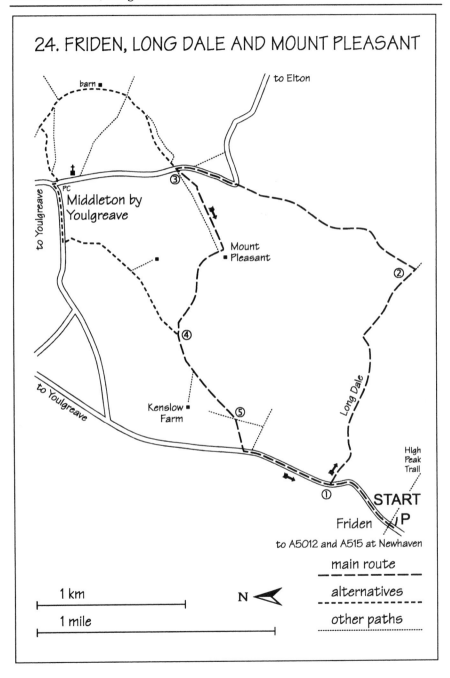

barn ■

to Elton

PC

Middleton by
Youlgreave

to Youlgreave

③

Mount
■ Pleasant

②

④

to Youlgreave

Long Dale

Kenslow ■
Farm

⑤

High
Peak
Trail

①

START

Friden **P**

to A5012 and A515 at Newhaven

main route
- - - - - -

N ◀

alternatives
- - - - - - - - - - -

1 km

other paths
....

1 mile

When you reach the top of the slope, continue along the clear path following the dale edge for a quarter of a mile to an iron gate on your left **(2)**, just before the path drops towards the dale bottom. Go through the gate and along the field, with the wall on your right, towards a ruined corrugated iron building. Follow the clear track, which here bends right and then left again and continues down the valley. After another quarter mile the right of way goes through an iron gate just to the left of the track, to pass down a walled path to the road.

On reaching the narrow road go straight on for a quarter mile until you pass a ruined building built into a rockface on the left. Shortly after this you will come to footpath signs on both sides of the road **(3)**. (The alternative route diverges here; or if you want the quickest way to the bus stop in Middleton-by-Youlgreave, go straight on up the road). Take the path on the left, onto a farm track. The right of way does not in fact follow the track, but diverges to the left to pass over a series of stiles in the direction of Mount Pleasant Farm which can be clearly seen ahead. Just before the farm turn right, keeping the wall on your left and ignoring a gate in it, onto a less-used (but clear) track which forks off the main track and goes through a gate. Beyond the gate the path turns left, alongside a wooded valley. After another gate it bends left, and a lane from Middleton joins from the right **(4)**.

Just beyond the next gate, leave the farm track at a footpath sign and follow the direction it indicates, diagonally across a field. Follow this direction across two ruined walls to an inconspicuous stile in the next wall, and on to another stile in the top corner of the next field to join a fenced track, not shown on the OS map **(5)**. Follow this track a few metres left to a gate leading into a large field. There is no visible path, but the right of way leads diagonally across it to a stile in the middle of the top wall, which brings you onto the road. Now turn left along the road for half a mile to return to the Friden car park.

Alternative routes

A very pleasant alternative route takes in Middleton-by-Youlgreave, an attractive little village built round an open square. The route is best when the leaves are off the trees, and is usable in most weather though there will be muddy patches after heavy rain. The route is about 6 miles.

Follow the route described down Long Dale and over the hill to the road, and walk down it; but instead of turning left up the Mount Pleasant track **(3)**, go over the stile on the other side of the road. The OS map shows the right-of-way climbing up the dale side opposite, then turning left along the dale edge; but the route which is evidently more used, and provided with good stiles, is along the bottom of the wooded dry dale to your left. The first stile is at the end of a cross-wall close to a rock face, and beyond this there is a clear stony path. The dale is narrow with rocky sides, though these are almost hidden by vegetation in summer.

Where the wood ends and the dale opens out, cross a wooden stile and continue ahead. Ignore a stile on the right; this is where the right-of-way along the dale edge rejoins the route. The path runs beside a tiny stream, often dry. When it reaches a farm track at a step stile (just left of the dale bottom) go straight across, with a wall on your right. Beyond a ruined barn the way is visible as a green path crossing several fields and step stiles, and bending gradually left towards a pine wood on a hillside. By an electricity pole the path drops to a stone slab bridge and turns left, climbing above the rim of an overgrown rocky dale (the upper end of Bradford Dale) and then dropping into it down an iron staircase and stone steps (with some fine fossil plant stems in them).

Cross the footbridge, and at a path junction turn left up another rocky track – this was the route from Middleton village to its corn mill. Entering the village, turn right to the square and very shortly left up the Newhaven road. Shortly beyond the last houses, where the road runs into a wood, take a narrow tarmac lane (Whitfield Lane) on the left. Go straight on past a farm drive on the left. Where the path goes through a gate it drops into a shallow dale and meets a cross track **(4)**; turn right with the main track. You are now back on the main route of the walk.

For a shorter walk of about 3 miles, park in Middleton-by-Youlgreave or take the bus there, and follow the first alternative route along Whitfield Lane, past the farm entrance, and the gate where it drops into the head of a dale **(4)**. Here turn left instead of right, through an iron gate and along a well-made track through a wood. At another gate the track turns right, in front of Mount Pleasant farm. The gravel farm drive leads to the road, but the right of way is rather to its right, over a series of stiles, before reaching the road at the same point as the drive. At the road **(3)**, go straight across and turn left down the dale; you are now back on the first alternative route, which will bring you back to Middleton-by-Youlgreave.

```
┌─────────────────────────────────────────────────────────────────────────┐
│                                                                           │
│              Walk 25: Elton and Gratton Dale                              │
│                                                                           │
└─────────────────────────────────────────────────────────────────────────┘
```

Start: At the church (SK222610) in Elton, five miles west of Matlock. There is
                    no car park, but you can park by the kerbside in the main street (but not
                    in front of the inn unless you are a customer).

                    Alternatively, park on the verge of the Winster road near where it
                    branches from the A5102 Newhaven to Cromford road (SK207593) at
                    point **(4)**.

Distance: 4 miles (alternative 5, or 3½ if you can find a parking place)

Public transport: There are five buses a day on a roundabout Matlock to Bakewell route,
                    calling at Elton in each direction; there is no Sunday service.

Amenities: The Duke of York in Elton does not offer meals, and its hours are irregular,
                    but there is a cafe just up the lane beside the inn.

                    There are inns and cafes in Winster, Hartington and Youlgreave, and also
                    toilets in each of these villages.

                    There is a picnic place at Elton Moor Lane at its T junction with the Winster
                    road, about a mile due south of the village (just off the sketch map).

The walk starts in the quiet village of Elton and descends across the
fields to the hamlet of Dale End, with good views across to Harthill
Moor. It then goes up Gratton Dale towards Mouldridge Grange, briefly
joins the road, and returns across the fields of Elton Moor to the village.

Gratton Dale is one of the lesser known dales, although I was surprised by the number of walkers on my last visit. It is usually dry
although there may be a small stream after wet weather. The path across
Elton Moor is well known to local people but little used by others.

There are 200 metres of road walking, along a busy road with a grass
verge, and a few more metres along quiet minor roads. Parts of the route
may be muddy after rain.

Elton lies close to the boundary between limestone and the area of
Millstone Grit which forms Harthill Moor to the north, with a narrow
band of softer shale between. The difference in scenery is notable, and
the underlying rock is most easily determined by looking at the stone
walls – pale grey limestone, often knobbly in this area, or dark reddish-
brown grit. Walling stone was, until recently, always quarried locally
and never carried far.

Elton

The Walk

Walk down Well Street, to the left of the church, and shortly fork left along a lane at a footpath signpost (to Youlgreave). Where the lane bends right, go straight ahead through an iron gate between two houses. Go a few metres to your left, past a redundant squeezer stile, to a footpath signpost, and then go half right down the field in the direction indicated by an arrow on the post rather than the arms of the signpost. From here there is a good view of Harthill Moor, with Youlgreave hidden beyond it.

You will soon see two squeezer stiles at the bottom of the field. Go through the left-hand one, in the middle of the wall. Continue along a green path to the corner of the field and cross the stile onto the road **(1)**.

Turn right along the road for a few metres and then go left over a step stile beside a gate. Follow the wall on the left through an open gateway and then over an iron gate, which was in a poor state when I last passed it. Continue along a visible green path through three narrow squeezer stiles, the third of these with a waymark post. Go slightly right, with the wall on your right, and you will find the next squeezer hidden beside

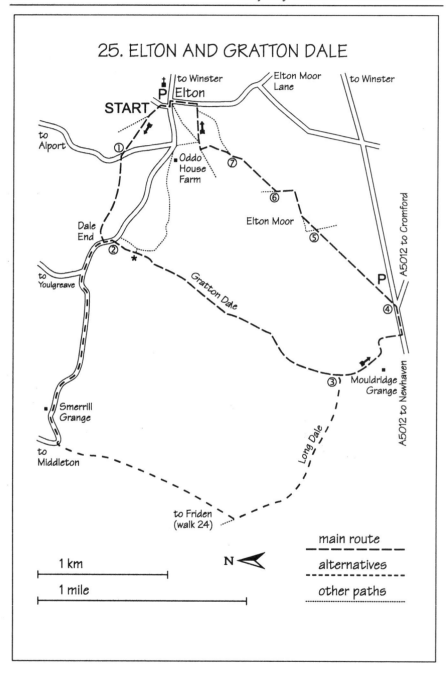

25. ELTON AND GRATTON DALE

to Winster

Elton Moor Lane

to Winster

P Elton

START

to Alport

①

Oddo House Farm

⑦

⑥

Elton Moor

⑤

A5012 to Cromford

Dale End

②

*

to Youlgreave

Gratton Dale

P

④

to Friden (walk 24)

③ Mouldridge Grange

A5012 to Newhaven

Smerrill Grange

to Middleton

Long Dale

1 km

1 mile

N

main route

alternatives

other paths

a gate, with a wooden stile in a wire fence just beyond (this may be temporary).

Bear rather to the left across the field to a pair of stiles in the far corner, by a hawthorn bush, then left along the wall to the next stile and diagonally through mud across an overgrown narrow field to the road; turn left along it for a few metres into the hamlet of Dale End. The last few metres before the road can be very wet; you may be able to avoid this to the right, but after very wet weather it would be wiser to take the quiet road from Elton to Dale End. (There is an alternative path by Oddo House Farm, but this runs largely through the farmyard so is not recommended).

Go through the squeezer beside the telephone box **(2)**, with a footpath sign, to enter Gratton Dale. The track up the dale is obvious. It may be muddy where the cows have churned it up, but most of the mud can be avoided. There is an old limekiln (with an information board) beside the next gate, and at the one after a notice tells you that English Nature is taking steps to thin out the scrub on the dale sides. The dale sides are smoother than those of other dales nearby but there is some rock, and in a few places the rock is not limestone; you are still close to the boundary between this rock and the shale and millstone grit.

The dale sides are at first largely covered by scrub, but later this gives way to grass and there are one or two plantations.

In just over a mile the dale divides **(3)**, and the path goes through a narrow wooden gate. Long Dale, to the right, leads to Friden; but ignore the gate into it and go straight on up the dale, on a clear path. You get only a glimpse of the farm buildings of Mouldridge Grange up a small side valley. The path leads through an open gateway and bears left alongside a wall. Where the wall bends to the right, keep alongside it to reach the A5012 road at a waymark post.

Turn left along the road for 200 metres; the traffic is fast, but there is a grass verge. At the fork **(4)**, the main road veers right while the minor road to Winster (where you could park on the verge) goes straight ahead. Take the stile by an iron gate on the left at the fork, with a footpath signpost 'Elton 1 mile' (actually it is more like a mile and a half) and go half right, in the direction pointed by the signpost. The path now runs dead straight for the best part of a mile, though a succession of stiles (one, hard to see from a distance, is just right of two large concrete troughs). Some of these large fields may have been sown with crops or new grass; you are entitled to follow the right of way straight across them, and you will probably find a visible path where others have done so before you.

Where you reach a firm track **(5)**, the way is still straight ahead across the field beyond; you should be able to see a footpath signpost beyond it, pointing towards you. When you reach it you will find it is on another firm track, and for a short way the footpath (signposted) follows this to the right and round a left-hand bend. Just past the bend, go over a stile on the right (with a footpath signpost) **(6)** and half-left to resume your original direction. Aim straight towards a distant television mast or, if it is not clear enough to see that, past an electricity pole which is rather to the left of the conical top of a grain silo. The path is clear on the ground. Beyond the pole you cross a wooden stile and bear slightly left, alongside a fence on your right, down the hill – aiming for a white house to the right of Oddo farm – till you reach a stile and footpath sign on your right **(7)**.

Cross the stile and turn left along a walled path. A stone stile on your right will take you across the fields to rejoin the walled route at a footpath sign just before it reaches the road, but it is simpler to go on down the walled path unless it has become very overgrown or muddy. It reaches a firmer walled track at a T junction; turn right. Shortly you will come to signs offering a choice of three ways into Elton. The easiest is to go straight on until you reach the road, then turn left for the few metres back to the church.

Alternative routes

For a rather longer walk (about 5 miles), after walking up Gratton Dale and through the narrow gate **(3)**, turn right through another narrow gate and walk up Long Dale. In rather under a mile the path ascends the dale side to the right. Go through an iron gate on the right and along the field, with the wall on your right, towards a ruined corrugated iron building. Follow the clear track, which here bends right and then left again and continues down the valley. After another quarter mile the right of way goes through an iron gate just to the left of the track, to pass down a walled path to the road. If this is too overgrown, follow the farm track to the road.

On reaching the narrow road, turn right along it for a mile and a half back to Elton: or take the path you came by from Dale End. You can reduce the length of this alternative to about 3½ miles if you can find a safe parking spot at the roadside at Dale End or to the west of it, but this may be difficult on summer Sundays.

Walk 26: High Peak Trail and Cobblersnook Lane

Start: At the Minninglow car park (SK145582) on the High Peak Trail. This car park is in fact a good mile from Minninglow Hill. It is reached by a minor road south from the A5012 Cromford to Newhaven road at Pike Hall.

Distance: 4¼ miles (alternatives 2½ miles, 4¾ miles)

Public transport: None close to the route. You can use the infrequent bus service along the A515 Ashbourne to Buxton road (see walk 24), alighting at the turn for Biggin and walking along Cardlemere Lane from there, but this will add two miles to your walk.

Amenities: There are several inns and cafes in Hartington and in Winster, but the Newhaven Inn and the Jug and Glass a little further north alng the A515 are both closed at the time of writing. There is a picnic site at the Friden car park (SK172607) on the High Peak trail, just over a mile beyond where this walk leaves it.

The nearest public toilets are at the former Hartington station, about three miles north-west of the Minninglow car park.

The walk explores a little known part of the White Peak, making use of part of the High Peak Trail and of some pleasant walled tracks. It is fairly level and mostly firm underfoot, though there are one or two muddy stretches. There is no road walking. The walk will be of interest to those

Cobblersnook Lane

interested in industrial remains, although most of it is through unspoilt country.

Half the walk is on the High Peak trail, a path for walkers, cyclists and horses, which follows the route of the old Cromford and High Peak railway. This was an interesting line, built in the 1820s to connect the Cromford Canal a few miles south of Cromford with the Peak Forest Canal at Whaley Bridge, by way of the outskirts of Buxton. It consisted of level stretches, worked originally by horses but later by locomotives, linked by steep inclines worked by cables driven by stationary steam engines. One of these engines has been preserved, at Middleton Top near Wirksworth, and is open to the public infrequently. This part of the line closed in the 1960s; booklets about it can be found in local bookshops and information centres.

The sketch map is drawn with East at the top.

The Walk

Walk westwards, over the road bridge, along the trail for about a mile, passing the very sharp Gotham curve about half way. This was said to be the sharpest curve on a standard-gauge railway in the country, and caused some difficulty to steam trains (the horses presumably had no problems with it). Where a walled track crosses the trail on the level **(1)**, turn left along it. This is Green Lane, and can be rather muddy. It dips at first, and then rises steadily.

Ignore a footpath which crosses the lane. At the top of the hill your lane comes to a T junction with another walled track **(2)**. To your right it is Cardlemere Lane, leading to Biggin; to the left, Cobblersnook Lane. Turn left along it. It is drier underfoot than the lane you have just left. The track passes through several gates. Where the way starts to drop, the wall on the left ends; continue down the field with a wall on your right. Ahead you can see Minninglow hill, crowned by a rather sparse clump of trees, with the route of the High Peak trail crossing the view like a very substantial stone wall.

The track becomes walled again and joins a firmer walled track at a gate; bear left along it to reach the road just beyond a cottage **(3)**. You can turn left here, reaching the car park in a quarter of a mile (making the walk about 2½ miles), but the main route continues straight ahead along Minninglow Lane. At a junction in about a third of a mile **(4)**, ignore the turning on the right and go straight on. In 200 metres ignore the track which turns left to a farm, and go straight ahead down the hill

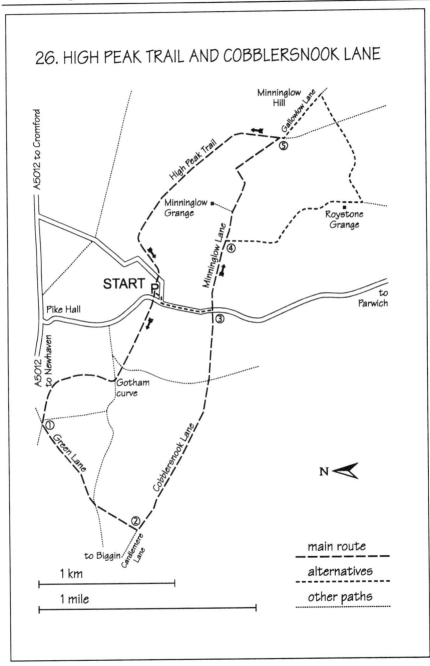

26. HIGH PEAK TRAIL AND COBBLERSNOOK LANE

main route

alternatives

other paths

and past a pond on your right. The lane swings left and then appears to be blocked by a wall, but in fact turns sharp right through a gate. On your left you can see the massive stone embankment of the old railway, now the High Peak Trail. The track passes through a gate onto the trail **(5)**. Turn sharp left along it, passing a well preserved Victorian limekiln and a disused quarry with an old crane, to return to the car park in another mile.

Alternative routes

A shorter alternative, about 2½ miles, is included in the description of the main walk.

If you are interested in archaeology you may like to visit Roystone Grange, which will add about half a mile to the walk; but you would be wise to get the 'Roystone Grange trail' leaflet beforehand from one of the Peak Park information centres to make the most of this. It describes the route in the opposite direction to that taken here.

Follow the main route as it crosses the road into Minninglow Lane as described above, then turn right at a junction **(4)** in a third of a mile into a lane which leads past Roystone Grange. A hundred metres or so beyond the farm, take a footpath on the left which climbs to a bridge under the High Peak trail. You cannot join the trail here without scrambling, so continue to a walled lane (Gallowlow Lane, a continuation of Minninglow Lane) and turn left along it. This brings you back to the trail **(5)**; turn right along it to reach the car park in about a mile.

Walk 27: Bonsall Moor

Start: Park on the very broad grass verge about 200 metres north of Slaley on the Upper Town road, near a footpath signpost (SK274577). Slaley is half a mile south-west of Bonsall, which is a mile west of Matlock Bath.

Although there is ample parking space here, the lanes leading to Slaley are very narrow (the best approach is from Winster direct, rather than via Upper Town). So you may prefer to park in a layby (with bird tables!) on the north side of A5012 at SK265566, about 300 metres on the Cromford side of the junction with the Wirksworth road, B5023. This adds little to the distance. If you park here, walk about 70 metres west along the road and go beside a gate on the right, and up a narrow valley (there is no signpost). In about 200 metres the main route joins from the right **(3)**; continue forward along it.

It is also possible to park where the route (on Blakemere Lane) crosses the very straight minor road from Winster to Slaley at SK255584. Park well onto the verge as the cross track is used by mine lorries.

If you are taking the alternative route via Bonsall village you can park there, either at the roadside in 'The Dale', a turning west off the main street opposite a bus shelter about 250 metres below the Cross (SK279580), or else in the car park a little further down on the other side of the street.

Distance: 4 miles (alternatives 3 and 5 miles).

Public transport: On weekdays (including Saturday) there is a bus every hour or two from Matlock to Bonsall which continues to Upper Town, a few hundred metres from the route. There is no Sunday service. For the stronger walker, it is about a mile from Matlock Bath station to Bonsall; but this includes a fair amount of ascent and descent.

Amenities: The King's Head in Bonsall and the Pig of Lead at the junction of the Bonsall road with the Via Gellia advertise food, although I have not tried them. There are various pubs and cafes in Matlock, Matlock Bath, Cromford and Wirksworth.

There are toilets in Bonsall just off the main street in 'The Dale' (see above), beyond a small workshop.

Bonsall Cross

This walk explores part of Bonsall Moor, which forms a salient of the Park boundary near to Matlock. The moor is farmed, almost entirely as sheep pasture, but the first part of the walk is along the brink of the heavily wooded Griffe Grange Valley down which runs the A5012 road, known as the 'Via Gellia' after a former landowner, Philip Gell.

Bonsall Moor was rich in lead and you will pass many relics of former mining. Some of the mined areas have been reworked recently by open-cast methods, for spar, and this continues.

The walk is entirely on limestone. The return path down Horse Dale may be muddy in places; but the worst mud can be avoided, and a drier alternative route is suggested. Views in the wooded section will be restricted when the leaves are on the trees, though the Griffe Grange valley is so heavily wooded that even in winter you can hardly see into it.

The main walk is within the Peak Park; the suggested starting point is on the boundary. About half a mile is on a quiet road. The extension to Bonsall village is outside the Park.

My sketch map is drawn with East at the top.

The Walk

Walk south to the road junction in the hamlet of Slaley and turn right. At the telephone box **(1)** fork left down a walled footpath beside a cottage. Go through the squeezer and half right to the far corner of the field. Go through the stile on the left beside an iron gate and turn right. The map shows the right of way close to the wall; but this is overgrown, so walk just below the bushes. Ignore a stile on the right leading to a barn, but pass a mound at the end of the field and go through the squeezer beyond it. Go straight on, alongside the wall on your left, to the next squeezer and on with the wall now on your right. The Griffe Grange Valley is on your left, but it is so heavily wooded that you can see very little of it. You pass the first of many signs of mining; several run-in shafts, including one where the top of the stone lining can be seen. The shaft is tiny, just wide enough for a miner to climb down.

At the end of the field the path goes through bushes into a rocky and rather muddy wood where it is joined by a path from the right **(2)**. Bear to the left for a short way ; you will see the path clearly ahead but it appears to be blocked by a fence. However you can get round the end of this, and cross a little stream by stepping stones. This is Dunsley

27. BONSALL MOOR

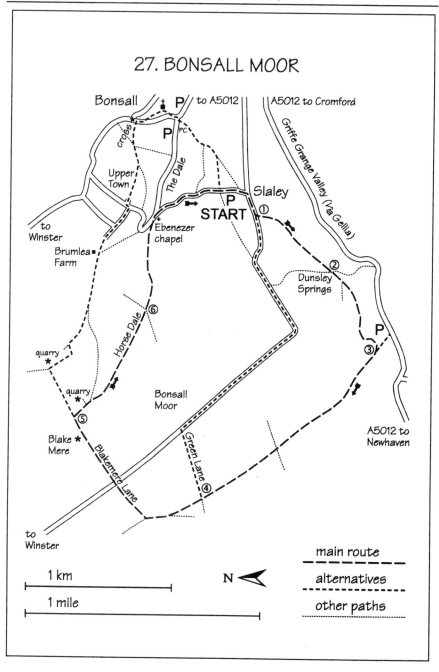

main route

alternatives

other paths

1 km

1 mile

N

Springs, and there are troughs either side of the path. Shortly the path forks; take the lower branch, which runs more or less level, rather than the broader one which slopes uphill. The path soon becomes clearer, between scrub on the right and a wall on the left, and runs along a level green terrace. There is more evidence of mining here.

At the end of the field the path goes between a fine pair of limestone posts and zigzags steeply downhill past a quarry tip, before becoming broader and less steep as it curves to the right into a side valley. Where it joins a path coming up the valley **(3)**, turn right (or left to return to your car if you parked at the layby on the Via Gellia). A clear stony path climbs up the valley, through a wood. A mossy wall runs up the valley on your left, and there are many wild flowers in spring.

Eventually the trees thin and the slope eases. Now go straight on for nearly a mile through a series of stiles, always keeping within twenty metres or so of the wall on your left, and leaving a large farm to your right. As you come towards the skyline some of the stiles are not easy to see from a distance, but if you keep straight ahead you will find them.

Where the path reaches a walled track (Green Lane) **(4)**, go left for a few metres and then right over a wooden stile (footpath signpost) and on alongside the wall until you reach another walled track (Blakemere Lane). Turn right along it, and follow it as it bends right. The ground on your right is heavily disturbed by mining. Continue across a minor road (you could park here) to the bottom of the valley; a reedy patch on your left is all that remains of Blake Mere.

Just beyond the overhead cables **(5)**, turn right along a muddy track (or walk on the grass alongside). Where the track turns left into a small active quarry, go straight on along a lesser gravel track. This bears right into Horse Dale. Bear left down the dale. Shortly the dale bottom is blocked by a cross wall; go to the right of this and you will find a clear path with stiles and the occasional waymark post, leading down the right-hand side of the valley. Where it comes to a small ruined building (probably associated with an old mine) and a post indicating a choice of ways **(6)**, go over the stile to the right of the ruin and on along the valley. You will pass several capped mine shafts, and the steep little village of Upper Town comes into sight.

When you reach buildings, go through the iron gate and along the walled lane to the road. Bear right, and beyond the little Ebenezer chapel fork right up a narrow road. You will be back at the starting point in about a quarter of a mile.

Alternative routes

An alternative route, about a mile longer, takes you into the attractive village of Bonsall. It is firm underfoot, apart from a muddy patch at Brumlea Farm and another on the path back to Slaley. To take this route, when you have passed Blake Mere do not turn into the track on the right **(5)** but continue ahead up the hill. Where this well-used track divides, fork right (the way has changed since the OS map was made because the quarry has been extended). Follow the track round a bend, with the quarry tip on your left, to a T junction and turn right along an older walled lane.

In about half a mile you pass Brumlea farm and the lane becomes tarmac. Ignore the first road junction, and continue to a T junction (and bus stop) at Upper Town. You could return to your starting point by turning right down the hill (fork right beyond the Ebenezer chapel for Slaley, or continue down the valley for 'The Dale'), but to see Bonsall village turn left, and then in a few metres turn right into a narrow road between houses. At the end of the lane go ahead through a squeezer into a walled footpath. From here the path is very clear, sometimes walled and sometimes through narrow fields, aiming towards the church spire until eventually it bears left and drops steeply, with steps in places, to the main street near Bonsall Cross.

The tall village cross stands on a stepped circular plinth in front of the King's Head, just to your left; but your way is to the right, down the main street. The cottages on the left back onto a limestone cliff. A short way down the road a pleasant path leads up to the churchyard – a branch right from it, down steps, brings you back to the road at the junction of 'The Dale'.

Cross the road into 'The Dale' (you could park here, and the toilets are a few metres up on the left) and immediately go left through a squeezer into a walled path (with a signpost), which climbs the hillside by steps. A squeezer takes you into a narrow field and a clear though muddy path slants across it and then bears left towards the skyline. Do not go through the gap in the cross wall here, but go through a squeezer high up on your right. Follow the hedge on your left to a wall gap, and continue close to the wall on your left. Go through a gateway straight ahead (or the squeezer beside it) and then through a squeezer on the right, and diagonally across the field to a squeezer just right of a double electricity pole. Now go half left across a narrow field to a squeezer, and then along the field through several more squeezers to reach the road at the suggested starting point. If you parked anywhere else, turn left along the road into Slaley, on the main route.

For a shorter walk of just over three miles, when you reach Green Lane turn right along it instead of going over the stile on the other side. In a quarter of a mile you will reach a quiet road. Turn right along it to return to Slaley in about a mile.

There are many other paths on Bonsall Moor, which you can follow if you have the 1:25000 OS map (you may find the occasional diversion because of mineral working). The Via Gellia, which is heavily wooded, makes a pleasant drive except for a couple of short industrial stretches: but don't try to walk it. The road is busy, and for most of the way there is no verge or footway.

Walk 28: Alsop Moor

Start: At the large layby (a bend cut out of the road) at SK156563 on the east side of A515 at the turning for Alsop Moor Cottages, a quarter mile south of the turning to Biggin.

If you are including Parwich in your walk you could park there, carefully at the roadside or in the car park by the recreation ground beyond the Sycamore Inn.

If you use the alternative route along the Tissington Trail you can park at the former Alsop station just off the A515 (SK155549): there is a small charge. There are picnic tables here, but no toilets.

Distance: 4 miles (alternatives 4 to 5).

Public transport: On Thursdays and Saturdays only there are one or two buses from Ashbourne to Parwich, Alsop-en-le-Dale and Alsop Moor.

Amenities: The Sycamore Inn near the church in Parwich serves food, and there are pubs and cafes in Hartington, Alstonefield and Ashbourne. A farm just south of the Alsop Station car park offers meals – you can reach it from the road or the Tissington Trail. The former Newhaven Inn, near the junction of the A515 and A5012, and the Jug and Glass a little further north on the A515 were both closed when I last saw them.

There are picnic sites at the former Alsop station (SK 155549) and at other former stations on the Tissington Trail.

There are toilets at the Tissington Trail car parks at the former Tissington and Hartington stations, and in Hartington, Alstonefield and Ashbourne. There are also toilets at Milldale in the Dove valley, but parking there is more difficult.

The walk starts on the A515, crosses Alsop Moor and descends through Eaton Dale to meet the road near Parwich. It then turns back over a spur of the moor and drops into the tiny village of Alsop-en-le-Dale, before climbing back to the starting point. This is almost entirely a walk through green fields, with a hundred metres along the broad verge of a main road and about two hundred on a quiet byroad. There is also a short length of the Tissington trail (more on the alternative routes): this is the former Ashbourne to Buxton railway which is now an all weather path for walkers, horse riders and cyclists. It is very popular with silent cyclists – you have been warned!

Alsop-en-le-Dale church

The walk is mostly on limestone, although little rock will be seen –
Eaton Dale is a grassy valley. About half a mile is on the overlying clay.
There are few muddy patches so it should be reasonable in all weathers.
Most of the walk is fairly level, but there are a couple of short steep
slopes.

Alsop-en-le-Dale consists of no more than the church, the Hall, two
large farms and a few cottages; but it is an attractive spot. The main walk
stops short of Parwich. If you have the time and strength it is worth the
extra mile needed to look at this pleasant village and, if it suits you, the
Sycamore Inn.

The map is drawn with East at the top, and details of Parwich village
are omitted for clarity.

The Walk

Before you leave the layby, notice the row of semi-detached villas –
Alsop Moor Cottages – planted incongrously in the middle of the fields.
They will serve as a landmark on the return journey.

From the top of the layby, cross the main road to a gate and walk up
onto the embankment of the Tissington Trail. Turn right along it. In a
few hundred metres the trail crosses a road bridge; just before it, take
the path branching left to the road and turn right along it. At the main
road turn left, and in a hundred metres cross to a quarry entrance (with
a footpath signpost) and go over the stile beside the gate **(1)**.

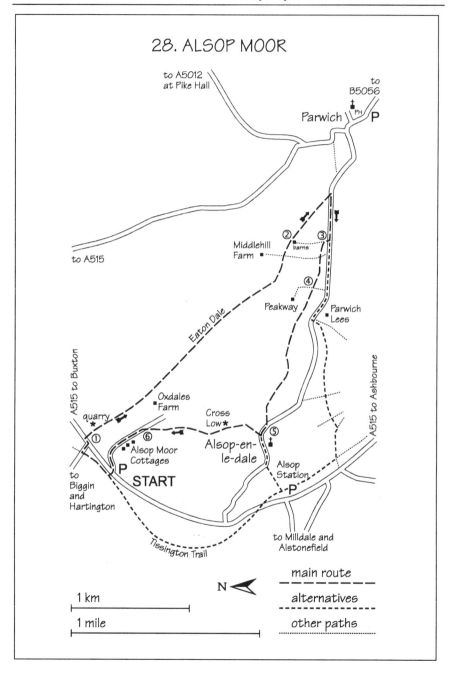

28. ALSOP MOOR

to A5012
at Pike Hall

to
B5056

Parwich ⌶ PH **P**

② ③
Middlehill
Farm ▪ barns

to A515

④

Peakway   Parwich
▪ Lees

Eaton Dale

A515 to Buxton

Oxdales
▪ Farm   Cross
Low★

A515 to Ashbourne

quarry
★
① ⑥   **Alsop-en-**
▪ Alsop Moor   ⑤
Cottages   **le-dale**
P   Alsop
Station
to   **START**   **P**
Biggin
and
Hartington

to Milldale and
Alstonefield

Tissington Trail

N ◀

main route
- - - - - - -

alternatives
· · · · · · ·

other paths
∙∙∙∙∙∙∙∙∙∙∙

1 km
├─────────┤

1 mile
├─────────┤

In a few metres cross another stile and turn left alongside the fence and quarry tip. You can now see four squeezers in a straight line. Go through them, and through a fifth, and on up the hill with the wall on your right. Where it bends, go slightly right to a fragmentary step stile just left of a gate. Carry on with the wall on your right, passing Oxdales Farm. Where the wall turns right, go straight ahead and go through the obvious gateway which you see as you come over the brow of the hill. Ahead of you the ground dips into Eaton Dale, and beyond the next gate you can see that the dale widens into a green bowl before narrowing again. On the flanks of the narrow part are the ridges of medieval farming, and you will see more in the next mile or so.

Carry on down the bottom of the dale, but where it opens out again keep slightly to the right, just below the trees, to a stile and waymark post about fifty metres to the right of the gateway with its little pond. Bear to the right, round the bottom of the slope, to a wall gap and waymark post by the slight ruins of a barn. By now you have clay underfoot. Aim slightly left towards an iron gate in the far corner of the field, with another waymark post, and go over the step stile beside it. Go ahead for a few metres and through a squeezer to the right of a gate.

Go straight ahead across the field, aiming for a group of barns in the middle distance. As you come over the brow of the hill you will see Middlehill farm to your left, and a wall in the dip ahead; the next step stile is over this wall in the far corner of the field. Cross the farm track, go through a squeezer under a tree and on to a wooden squeezer. Now aim for the left-hand end of the group of farm buildings **(2)**, turn right round the end of the concrete wall and go through a very narrow stone squeezer. The well-fed may have to make a short detour through two gates on the left.

Now turn fairly sharp left and make for the far corner of the field towards an obvious gate – beside it is a squeezer with its own little gate. Beyond it continue down the ridge, aiming towards a farm, and a barn will come in sight in the valley. Aim just right of it, and a squeezer beside a gate will bring you onto a quiet road.

If you want to visit Parwich turn left here (a short way on, a lane on the left with a footpath signpost shortens the distance slightly), then return to this point. The main route is to the right along the road for about 200 metres. You will pass a rocky outcrop which shows that you are back on the limestone. Before the first bend, at a wooden gate set back from the road there is a footpath signpost **(3)**. Go through the gate and turn left, almost parallel with the road. After a double stile, cross the farm track at a footpath signpost and go on through a squeezer hidden under a tree. Now go up the slope, diverging slightly from the fence on your left and passing to the right of a small tree which, as you come closer, you will find has a wooden fence round it.

The next stile, in a wooden fence, is hard to see from a distance; but if you aim for a pole in the dip on the horizon you will come to it **(4)**. Cross the stile, a drive, another wooden stile and a stone squeezer. Go just right of the stone building to another squeezer and on to the next, by an electricity pole. Now follow the track straight on up a slope through a fledgling plantation – the trees were about a metre high in 1996.

Go through the squeezer by the gate at the top of the wood and straight on, converging with the overhead cables, to a squeezer on the skyline. Continue through two more squeezers, keeping close to the wall on your left. On your right there is a limestone outcrop on the skyline; on your left a steep drop into the dale, and ahead you will soon see Alsop-en-le-Dale. Part way along the wall on your left is an inconspicuous step stile and signpost. Cross the stile and go diagonally across the field towards the village, over another step stile, and aim for the farm entrance. You will find a stile and steps leading down to the road. Turn right along the road into the village **(5)**.

Your route is up a farm track (signposted) on the right not far beyond the first cottage, but it is worth going on a few metres to look at the attractive buildings and the tiny church. This has an impressive Norman doorway; the 'Norman' tower and nave windows are in fact recent, as you will see from the 1895 photograph inside the church. Return to the signposted farm track.

The track leads through the end of a farmyard, but it is firm underfoot and should not be too muddy. Go straight on up the field to an electricity post with a waymark arrow, and then bear rather to the left and climb steeply to a squeezer just left of the cables. Carry on up the rocky field, which is full of flowers in the spring, to the skyline. On either hand is a walled clump of trees containing a mound, probably a prehistoric burial place. The mound on your right is called Cross Low, which suggests that it once carried a medieval cross which probably served as a direction post.

You will see a wall ahead of you. Walk left along it, and follow it round the corner to a squeezer. You can see Alsop Moor Cottages ahead and your way is towards the right-hand end of them, through an obvious gateway. As you come over the curve of the hill you will find four walls meeting, three of them standing in a little pond. Go through the two squeezers just left of the junction, and on towards a gate and squeezer at the far corner of the field. This brings you onto a tarmac lane **(6)**. Turn left, past the houses, and follow the lane back to the main road and the starting point.

Alternative routes

You can add a pleasant mile by continuing into Parwich, an attractive quiet village; return the same way to the main route. The village is built round a confusing network of lanes which I have not tried to show on the map, so don't get lost!

If you would like to see more of the Tissington Trail, at Alsop-en-le-Dale continue past the church for two hundred metres. Half way round a bend, at a footpath signpost, cross the combined wooden stile and squeezer on the left. Go up the hill with the wall on your right, ignoring the gate in it, till you reach a squeezer; go through it and continue uphill with the wall now on your left. Where the wall curves away, go straight ahead through a squeezer onto the Tissington Trail. (Alsop Station car park is just to your left). Turn right along the trail for about a mile to your starting point. This will add about half a mile to your walk.

Another alternative avoids Alsop-en-le-Dale village and the climb over the spur which precedes it. The distance is about four miles. To go this way, when you turn right along the road after walking down Eaton Dale, do not leave it at the gate on the right but continue for a further half mile, passing a large farm (Parwich Lees) on the left. Just before the bottom of the dip there is a two-armed footpath signpost on the left. Ignore the green lane going left, but go through the squeezer beside the iron gate on the other side of it and diagonally down the field, curving round the slope on your right, to a step stile in the far corner.

Walk up the valley to the next gateway (the stile is beside it) and climb gently along the foot of the steep slope on your left. Just above a row of hawthorns (with a good view of Alsop village) there is a wall corner; pass it and go half left up the hillside, aiming for a clump of trees on the skyline just left of a larger nearer clump. Go through a combined wooden stile and squeezer and on to a squeezer just left of the trees. Turn right to another squeezer, and then go diagonally left across the field aiming for an old railway bridge, via another squeezer. At the bridge, go over a step stile on the left and up steps to join the Tissington trail. Turn right along it. In a quarter of a mile you will pass the Alsop Station car park; keep on the trail and you will be back at your starting point in another mile.

Walk 29: Parwich to Tissington

Start: In Parwich village (SK188543). Either park at the roadside near the
                        church gate, or use the parking area by the sports field which is about
                        300 metres south-east along the Ashbourne road, beyond the green
                        opposite the Sycamore Inn.

                        Alternatively, use the large Tissington Trail car park at the former
                        Tissington station (SK177521); there is a small charge.

Distance: 4½ miles (alternative 3¾).

Public transport: There are a very few buses to Parwich from Ashbourne and Hartington
                        on Thursdays and Saturdays only, and Tissington also has a few buses
                        from Ashbourne on Thursday and Saturday only. On summer Sundays
                        a single bus on the Mansfield-Derby-Ashbourne-Buxton route, and one
                        on the Macclesfield-Buxton-Ashbourne route, call at Tissington Gates on
                        the main A515 road about half a mile from Tissington village; these buses
                        are timed to give a full day out.

Amenities: The Sycamore Inn, near the church in Parwich, normally has bar meals
                        lunchtime and evening although on our visit there was only cold food.
                        The Bluebell Inn, which also suppies food, is on the A515 just south of
                        Tissington Gates (the main turning for Tissington). Light refreshments
                        are sometimes obtainable in Tissington or at the Tissington car park, and
                        there are pubs at Fenny Bentley and at Thorpe crossroads, south and
                        south-west of Tissington. There are many pubs and cafes in Ashbourne.

                        There are toilets at the Tissington trail car park on the outskirts of
                        Tissington village, and in Ashbourne.

This walk is in the lush farming country in the south-east corner of the
park, mainly on red soil though the limestone is not far off to the north.
It is mainly hedge and fence country, but there are a few stone walls
and many stone squeezer stiles. The route may be wet near the two
crossings of the brook, so this is one for fairly dry weather or else a hard
frost. Most of the fields have not been treated with weedkiller and are
full of wild flowers in spring and summer.

Tissington is one of the show villages of the Peak District, with its
hall, church and cottages grouped about the village green and duck-
pond. It has the oldest of the well-dressing traditions (usually in
mid-May). It can be crowded at summer weekends. Parwich is less well

Parwich

known but is also attractive, with its own green and many pleasant cottages and larger houses, though the church is Victorian.

The paths are not much used, with few waymarks, but are unobstructed. There are several hills on the way, though none is very steep. Note that in one or two places the paths, as indicated by the stiles, are not quite as shown on the 1:25000 OS map.

The Walk

Turn left from the church gate, and left along the road past the Sycamore Inn. Where the road bends left beyond the houses on the right, turn right (at a footpath signpost) into a track just before the sports field – there is room to park here. Continue through the farmyard by three gates. Now go half left up the field towards its far left corner, and through the left-hand of the two gates there. Carry on in the same direction, aiming well to the left of the barn. Ignore a very prominent pair of stone gateposts but go through a gateway about 100 metres further left.

Now go straight up the field; ignore the gateway straight ahead of you

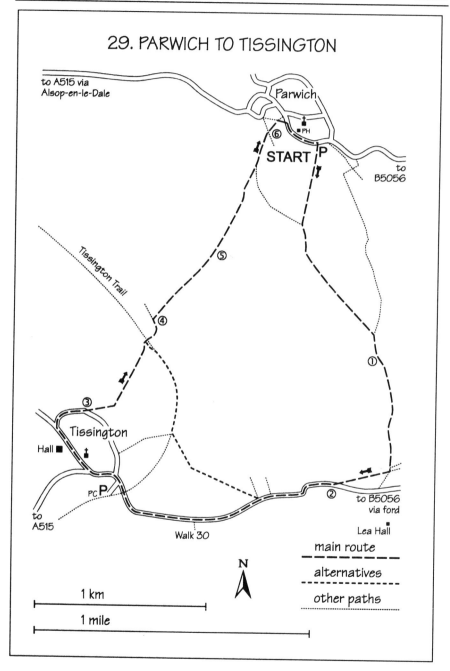

29. PARWICH TO TISSINGTON

to A515 via
Alsop-en-le-Dale

Parwich

■ PH

⑥

START P

to
B5056

⑤

Tissington Trail

④

①

③

Tissington

Hall ■   ☥

PC P

②   to B5056
via ford

to
A515

Walk 30   Lea Hall ■

N

main route

alternatives

1 km   other paths

1 mile

but bear a little to the left and go through a gateway near the end of the left wall. Follow the hedge and fence on your right to a wooden stile and go over it. Now go half left, just right of a large tree, and turn left just past it to follow the row of trees (an old hedge) on your left, keeping more or less level. Beyond a wooden stile carry on in the same direction with the fence now on your right. Carry on through a couple of stone squeezers, a wooden stile, and another beside a gate, and go down a long field to the iron gate which leads you to a level (and possibly wet) field in the valley bottom. Cross this to the far right corner, where you will find a plank bridge over the Bletch Brook under a large willow tree **(1)**.

Go straight ahead, aiming to the right of the farm and just to the left of a pair of isolated trees, to a wooden stile on the skyline. Over this, follow the fence until it turns left, and continue straight ahead through a gateway and on to a wooden stile with a stone squeezer just beyond it. Carry on, following the hedge on your right over the skyline, until you reach a field corner with a step stile and a waymark post beside an iron gate. Go over the stile and turn right alongside the hedge, along a very large field which has a large farm (Lea Hall) at its far side, on your left. Ignore the gate leading into a field on the right, and you will converge with an unfenced tarmac road (Bent Lane, which has come from Bradbourne Mill via a ford) at a footpath sign **(2)**.

Go over the cattle grid and along the road for two thirds of a mile, into Tissington village. Just before you enter the village you will go over the former railway line which is now the Tissington Trail. (The turning on the left just past the bridge takes you to the car park, picnic area and toilets). A short way beyond this, bear left at the first road junction and right at the next for the village centre. Walk up the road between the greens, and where it passes through a group of cottages take the narrow right fork (Chapel Lane), and follow it round a bend to the right.

In about 300 metres, where the road turns right, go straight ahead along a walled track **(3)**. After a third of a mile this crosses the Tissington Trail by a brick bridge. Continue over the bridge and round a bend, past a small plantation. Where the track straightens you should find a footpath signpost **(4)**. Leave the track here and walk down the field on the right towards a green hump, crossing a stone step stile to reach it. Carry on over the hump and towards the right-hand corner of the field, and go through a stone squeezer (with hinged flap) a few metres left of the corner.

Now go straight across the meadow to a small tree beside which a plank bridge takes you back across the Bletch Brook **(5)**; there may be mud here if the stone causeway has not been mended. Go straight on up the hillside, past a single electricity pole, to the top corner of the field where you will find a plank bridge, over a dry ditch, under a large tree. Go over this and turn left alongside the hedge. Beyond a squeezer beside a gateway, go ahead under the cables to a pair of trees and continue with the hedge on your left. Beyond a narrow squeezer you will have a good view of Parwich, with the church spire in the centre and a fine brick-built hall with terraced gardens to the left.

Bear slightly left to a squeezer just before a gate at the bottom of the left wall. Turn right alongside the wall, past the gate, and over a wooden stile in a wooden rail fence **(6)**. A fenced path leads you through two squeezers and emerges by a house gate onto a green with children's play equipment. For the church, follow the track to the road and turn left; for the sports field car park, turn right across the green and walk along the road past the Sycamore Inn.

Alternative routes:

If you have already visited Tissington you can miss out the village, and save three quarters of a mile. After joining Bent Lane near Lea Hall **(2)**, walk along it for about a quarter of a mile. Beside the second of two farm drives on the right is a waymark post; go over the cattle grid and half left across the large field as indicated by the post, aiming left of a clump of trees on the highest point and passing a stone drinking trough in the dip. As you go over the rise you will find a stile beside a gate and a round drinking trough. Go straight on, aiming just right of a barn, to a stile (with a waymark post) in a stone wall. Now go half right across the field to the nearer end of a stone wall, where you will find a notice board and a step stile which leads to wooden steps down to the Tissington Trail – a firm track which was once the Ashbourne to Buxton railway line.

Turn right along the trail, watching out for cycles which (along with horses) are also allowed to use the trail. In about a third of a mile you will see a bridge over the trail. Before you reach it, take a path on the left signed 'Tissington and Parwich'. This brings you to a farm drive. Turn right and follow it over the bridge; you are now back on the main route.

Walk 30: Tissington and Fenny Bentley

Start: At the car park on the Tissington Trail, at the south-east corner of Tissington village (SK 178521). There are toilets and picnic tables here; there is a small parking charge.

Alternatively, at the Thorpe car park on the Tissington Trail (SK166503), half a mile east of Thorpe village (if full, there is another car park nearby, nearer the crossroads). It is difficult to park where the route crosses the A515 at Fenny Bentley.

Distance: 4 miles (alternatives 3½ and 4½ miles)

Public transport: There is no regular weekday bus service, other than a school bus, but on Thursdays and Saturdays there are occasional buses from Ashbourne to Tissington village via Fenny Bentley, and to Ilam via the Dog and Partridge at Thorpe crossroads (on the alternative route, and about a quarter of a mile from the main route).

On Sundays a bus from Mansfield and Derby via Ashbourne, timed to give you a whole day out, calls at Thorpe crossroads and at Tissington Gates, on the A515 about half a mile from the village. On Sundays in summer only, there are two buses a day (one running through from Macclesfield) from Buxton to Ashbourne which pass Tissington Gates and Thorpe crossroads.

Amenities: There is no pub in Tissington, but the Bluebell Inn on the A515 just south of the Tissington turning ('Tissington Gates') provides food. The Coach and Horses on the A515 at Fenny Bentley (close to the route of the walk) and the Dog and Partridge at Thorpe crossroads also serve bar meals. There are many pubs and cafes in Ashbourne, and some on the A515 on the way there. A few local farms serve teas. Light refreshments are sometimes available at the Tissington car park, or in the village.

There are toilets at the Tissington car park, and in Ashbourne, but not at the Thorpe car park (the nearest are in Thorpe village, half a mile to the west).

This walk is among the lower hills at the southern tip of the Peak Park, where stone walls are replaced by hedges. It is mainly through fields. The final stage is along the firm path of the Tissington Trail, the former Ashbourne to Buxton railway. There are only a few hundred metres of road walking, on a quiet lane.

Ridge and Furrow near Tissington

The village of Tissington is one of the most attractive in the district, and its well-dressing ceremonies are among the few which have persisted without a break. It is a popular spot, especially during the week of the well-dressing when it may be wise to use the alternative parking place.

The walk should be reasonable in most weathers, but there may be a few muddy patches. After very wet weather, see the route suggested under 'alternatives'. Some of the stiles are rather narrow, although well maintained.

The whole walk is on the current 'White Peak' outdoor leisure map. Early editions were a quarter of a kilometre shorter, and if you have one of those you will find that Fenny Bentley is just off the map.

The Walk

From the Tissington car park, walk back to the road and turn right along it, away from the village. Cross the bridge and a cattle grid, go round a bend, and turn right along a tarmac farm road opposite a barn. There is no footpath sign, but this is a right of way – legally a public road, serving several farms. Follow it round a bend to the left, but where it turns sharp right leave it and go straight ahead through a gate **(1)**. A track leads across the field to a gate; go through it and straight on, to a gate in the far right corner of the field.

Carry on alongside the hedge on your right. Where the hedge turns right, follow it round to a stile and gate under an old tree. Go straight ahead, at first alongside the hedge and then, where the hedge turns, straight on across the field to two gates. From here there should be a good view across the valley of the Bentley brook, but as we walked in thick mist I cannot describe it for you. Go over the stile by the left-hand gate and on with the fence (which later becomes a hedge) on your right. Keep close to the hedge as it bends to the right. Cross a stile by a gate, then go rather to the right to a stile and gate just to the left of Lees Farm **(2)**.

Cross the farm track and go straight ahead across the field to a gate by an electricity pole. Bear just right of the cables to the next gate, and then to a twin stone squeezer stile by the next electricity pole. Follow the cables to the right of a stone barn, and continue alongside the hedge on your right to a squeezer stile with its own little gate, alongside a farm gate. Now follow the hedge on your left as it bends left, but when it turns very sharply left go straight ahead towards the spire of Fenny Bentley church. Pass a double electricity pole and a row of houses, and go through a squeezer to join a firm track.

Turn left along the track. On your left is Bentley Old Hall, which incorporates a medieval tower. The track reaches the A515 main road at the old school and telephone box. The Coach and Horses is a hundred metres to your left (leave your boots in the porch): but your way is a few metres to the right, across the road, and through the lychgate into the churchyard. Pass the church (which is largely Victorian outside, though it has older features) and join a lane. If you deviated to the pub, a path nearly opposite will take you past the school onto this lane.

Turn left along the lane, and just past the last house **(3)** turn right through a wicket gate, signposted to Thorpe. Go up the field and through another gate, keeping close to the hedge on your right. Beyond a stile in a wire fence, follow a faint path parallel to the hedge to an inconspicuous stile about twenty metres left of the hedge corner. Follow the hedge, now on your left, to the next stile.

At this point you could take a more direct path to the right; but this is muddy so go straight ahead to a footbridge over the stream, and on up the hillside until you meet the Tissington Trail **(4)**, a firm surfaced

30. TISSINGTON AND FENNY BENTLEY

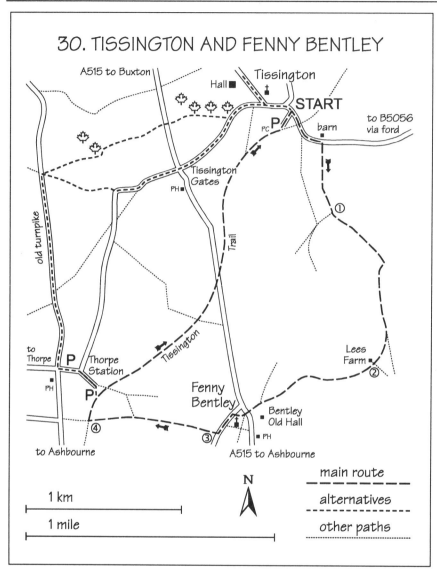

main route

N

1 km   alternatives

1 mile   other paths

path on the route of an old railway. The path is also open to horses and cycles, so take care. Turn right along it and you will soon come to the site of Thorpe station, where you will find picnic tables, a shelter and a car park though no toilets. (If you follow the car park drive to the road, and continue forward, you will come to the Dog and Partridge at Thorpe crossroads in about a quarter of a mile).

Continue along the Trail, which runs through a long cutting which now serves as a nature reserve. You cross the A515 on a high bridge, and the path curves through a further wooded cutting. It reaches the Tissington car park in about a mile and a half from the one at Thorpe.

Alternative routes

A walk to the end of Tissington village and back – about a quarter of a mile each way – is well worth while. The village is built round a green, with the Jacobean hall at one side of it and several wells (springs feeding troughs) which are dressed with flower pictures once a year, usually in late May. See 'Peakland Post' for the dates. The church is ancient, though the exterior is much restored. It contains a magnificent wall tomb and an interesting font.

If you want a change from railway trails, you can instead use the former turnpike north from Thorpe crossroads. This is now a very quiet rural lane, having been superseded by the A515. This route will add about half a mile to the distance.

Follow the main route to the Thorpe station car park, and take the car park access way to the road and on to Thorpe crossroads (by the Dog and Partridge). Turn right here, up the old turnpike (Spend Lane), and follow it for three quarters of a mile as it climbs onto the limestone, with good views behind you. After a short open stretch the road becomes walled again. About a quarter of a mile on, just before a group of hawthorn trees on the right of the road, go through a narrow stone squeezer on the right. There is a footpath signpost with two arms. Follow the direction of the left-hand one, slightly left across the field to the right-hand end of a tree belt. Go ahead, now dropping quite steeply, keeping close to the wall on your left. You may notice that the fields ahead and to the left of you have broad, gently curved ridges – seen particularly well when there is a little wind-blown snow on the ground; these are the remains of medieval 'ridge and furrow' ploughing with ox-teams. They have survived because the land became pasture and has not been ploughed in more recent times.

Cross a wooden stile and immediately a stone step stile, and go on a short way to a gateway on your left. Go through this, straight on past the end of a wall (with a redundant step stile), and turn right down the narrow field. At the far left corner you will find a slab bridge and then a stone squeezer with a waymark post. Go straight up the next field (or follow the ridges, which here have a double curve) to a footpath signpost on the skyline. Cross the main road carefully to a stile on the other side, then ignore the arm of the signpost and go half left to a stile beside an iron gate in a wire fence. Follow the tree belt on your left to another stile, beyond which you join an unfenced road running through an avenue of trees. You will notice that the road crosses more ploughing ridges, with the trees carefully planted on the crest of each ridge. Turn left along the road, keeping right at each junction, to return to the car park.

After heavy rain, a route which is firm underfoot for most of its length is to take the Tissington Trail southwestwards from Tissington to Thorpe station. Then follow the alternative route to Thorpe Crossroads and up the old turnpike as described above; leave it at the same point, but follow the right-hand arm of the signpost, passing to the right of the water trough, and walk parallel to the wall on your right. Where this turns away, go straight ahead towards the highest point on the skyline. When you are over the ridge you will see a road running straight away from you. Make for this, over two stiles both under large trees, and you will join the road at a corner. Turn left along the road, watching out for traffic. At the main road, go straight ahead between the gateposts ('Tissington Gates') and follow the unfenced road back to the village. Keep right at each junction for the car park. This route is about 3½ miles.

Bentley Old Hall